Study Guide for use with

Social Psychology

SECOND CANADIAN EDITION

David G. Myers
Hope College

Steven J. Spencer
University of Waterloo

Prepared by
Susan Hartley
Conestoga College

McGraw-Hill
Ryerson

Toronto Montréal Boston Burr Ridge, IL Dubuque, IA Madison, WI New York San Francisco
St. Louis Bangkok Bogotá Caracas Kuala Lumpur Lisbon London Madrid
Mexico City Milan New Delhi Santiago Seoul Singapore Sydney Taipei

**Study Guide for use with
Social Psychology
Second Canadian Edition**

ISBN: 0-07-093369-3

1 2 3 4 5 6 7 8 9 10 TRI 0 9 8 7 6 5 4

Printed and bound in Canada

Care has been taken to trace ownership of copyright material contained in this text; however, the publisher will welcome any information that enables them to rectify any reference or credit for subsequent editions.

Vice President, Editorial and Media Technology: Pat Ferrier
Sponsoring Editor: James Buchanan
Developmental Editor: Sandra de Ruiter
Marketing Manager: Sharon Loeb
Supervising Editor: Jaime Duffy
Production Coordinator: Andrée Davis
Printer: Tri-Graphic Printing

SOCIAL PSYCHOLOGY 2ce
MYERS/SPENCER

Study Guide Contents

Chapter 1   Introducing Social Psychology   1

Chapter 2   The Self in a Social World   19

Chapter 3   Social Beliefs and Judgments   35

Chapter 4   Behaviour and Attitudes   53

Chapter 5   Culture, Language, and Gender   70

Chapter 6   Conformity   87

Chapter 7   Persuasion   104

Chapter 8   Group Influence   121

Chapter 9   Altruism: Helping Others   138

Chapter 10   Aggression: Hurting Others   156

Chapter 11   Attraction and Intimacy: Liking and Loving Others   173

Chapter 12   Prejudice: Disliking Others   191

Chapter 13   Conflict and Peacemaking: Intergroup Relations   211

Module A   Social Psychology in the Clinic   226

Module B   Social Psychology in Court   242

Module C   Social Psychology and a Sustainable Environment   259

CHAPTER 1
INTRODUCING SOCIAL PSYCHOLOGY

CHAPTER OBJECTIVES

After completing your study of this chapter you should be able to:

1. Define social psychology and give examples of the discipline's central concerns.
2. Identify similarities and differences between social psychology and the other disciplines that study
   human nature.
3. Indicate how the personal values of social psychologists penetrate their work.
4. Discuss the nature and implications of the "hindsight bias" for social psychology.
5. Explain the general nature and purpose of a theory.
6. Describe two major research methods used in social psychology and state the advantages and disadvantages of each.
7. Identify ethical standards that govern social-psychological research.

CHAPTER REVIEW

Supply the words necessary to complete each of the following statements.

1. Social psychology is the _____ study of how people think about, _____, and relate to one another. It is still a _____ discipline with the first social psychology experiments being reported just a _____ ago.
2. Social psychology emphasizes the power of the _____, the power of the _____, the importance of _____, and how to apply the principles of _____.

SOCIAL PSYCHOLOGY AND RELATED DISCIPLINES

3. Most sociologists study _____, while social psychologists are usually interested in studying _____. Compared to the sociologist, the social psychologist makes greater use of the _____ method.

4. In contrast to personality psychology which focuses on _____ among individuals, social psychology focuses on how social situations can lead _____ _____ individuals to behave.

5. Every psychological event is simultaneously a biological event. Biology examines the _____ underlying social behaviour while social psychology examines the _____ influences.

6. The disciplines which study human nature provide different _____ of explanation that _____ rather than contradict one another.

SOCIAL PSYCHOLOGY AND HUMAN VALUES

7. Social psychologists' personal _____ penetrate their work in obvious ways like their _____ of research topics.

8. In addition there is a growing awareness that science is not as purely _____ as commonly thought. Scientists view their world through their _____ which control their interpretations. In addition, the _____ of scientists are hidden in the concepts, advice, and labels used in social psychology. Scientists are guilty of the _____ fallacy when they   define what is good in terms of what is observable.

I KNEW IT ALL ALONG: IS SOCIAL PSYCHOLOGY SIMPLY COMMON SENSE?

9. The _____ bias is the tendency to exaggerate one's ability to have foreseen how something turned out after learning the outcome and may explain why social psychology's findings often seem like _____
_____.

HOW WE DO SOCIAL PSYCHOLOGY

10. Social psychologists organize their ideas and findings into _____ that both explain and _____ observed events.

11. Most social psychological research is conducted either in the _____ or in the _____ and uses either the _____ or _____ method of research.

12. The great strength of correlational research is that it tends to occur in _____- _____ settings where it can examine important factors that cannot be _____ in the laboratory. Correlational research can tell us whether two variables are associated but cannot provide _____ and _____ explanations.

13. Survey researchers obtain a representative group by taking a _____ _____ in which every person in the total group has an equal chance of being chosen to participate. About _____ randomly selected participants will enable the researcher to be 95 percent confident of describing the entire population within an error margin of 3 percent or less. Three potentially biasing influences on surveys are _____ samples, the _____ of questions, and the _____ options.

14. Two essential ingredients of every social-psychological experiment are _____ and _____ assignment. Researchers often walk a tightrope in designing experiments that will be involving yet _____.

MATCHING TERMS

Write the letter of the correct term from the right before the appropriate number on the left.

_____ 1. A cue in an experiment that tells the participant what behaviour is expected.

_____ 2. The study of the naturally occurring relationships among variables.

_____ 3. An integrated set of principles that explains and predicts observed events.

_____ 4. Defining what is good in terms of what is observable.

_____ 5. Research done in natural, real-life settings outside the laboratory.

_____ 6. Placing participants in the conditions of an experiment such that each has an equal chance of being in a given condition.

_____ 7. Research participants must be told enough to enable them to choose whether they wish to participate.

_____ 8. Studies which seek clues to cause-effect relationships by manipulating one or more factors while controlling others.

_____ 9. Every person in the group has had an equal change of being chosen to participate in a study.

_____ 10. The tendency to exaggerate one's ability to have foreseen how something turned out, after learning the outcome.

_____ 11. Extent to which an experiment is superficially similar to everyday situations.

_____ 12. Extent to which an experiment absorbs and involves its participants.

_____ 13. Enduring behaviors and ideas shared by a large group of people and transmitted from one generation to the next.

a. naturalistic fallacy

b. random assignment

c. correlational research

d. mundane realism

e. random sample

f. experimental realism

g. hindsight bias

h. field research

i. experimental research

j. demand characteristic

k. informed consent

l. culture

m. a theory

TRUE-FALSE REVIEW

Circle T if the statement is true and F if it is false.

T   F   1. Most people would refuse to engage in acts of cruelty.

T   F   2. The first social psychology experiments were reported in the 1930s.

T   F   3. Contemporary social psychology emphasizes the power of the situation and downplays the contribution of the person to social behavior.

T   F   4. Contemporary social psychology recognizes the importance of cognition in understanding social behavior.

T   F   5. In comparison to sociologists, social psychologists are more interested in studying the individual.

T   F   6. Every psychological event is a biological event.

T   F   7. To the degree social psychologists are successful in explaining human behavior, other disciplines become less important.

T   F   8. Social psychology's ultimate goal is to explain the purpose of human life.

T   F   9. Social psychologists have investigated how values are formed and how they can be changed.

T   F   10. Social representations are our most important but least examined convictions.

T   F   11. Hidden value judgments are more common in psychology than in sociology.

T   F   12. The "I-Knew-It-All-Along" phenomenon provides one example of the naturalistic fallacy.

T   F   13. The findings of social psychology typically prove common sense ideas are wrong.

T   F   14. Hindsight bias is conducive to arrogance--an overestimation of our own intellectual powers.

T F 15. Theories are most frequently discarded because they have been falsified.

T F 16. A good theory makes clear predictions that can be used to confirm or modify the theory.

T F 17. The experimental method enables researchers to answer questions about causal relationships.

T F 18. The correlational method would be best to determine if wealth is related to health.

T F 19. There are at least three possible explanations for every correlational finding.

T F 20. A total of 1200 randomly selected participants will enable a survey researcher to be 95 percent confident of describing the entire population of a country with an error margin of 3 percent or less.

T F 21. The way in which questions are asked can influence respondents' answers in a survey.

T F 22. Random assignment is an important feature of well-done surveys.

T F 23. An example of a demand characteristic would be when an experimenter smiles whenever a subject gives an expected answer.

T F 24. An experiment has mundane realism if it absorbs and involves its participants.

T F 25. One ethical principle advocated by the Canadian Psychological Association is that investigators treat information about the individual research participants confidentially.

MULTIPLE-CHOICE PRACTICE TEST

Circle the correct letter.

1. Social psychology is the scientific study of how people _____,
   _____, and _____ one another.
   a. understand, feel about, act toward
   b. perceive, think about, act toward
   c. think about, influence, relate to
   d. observe, influence, conflict with

2. Social psychology began to emerge as the vibrant field it is today during
   a. the depression of the early 1930s when researchers examined the effects of deprivation on aggression and altruism
   b. world War I when psychologists conducted studies of social conflict and cooperation
   c. World War II when researchers performed studies of persuasion and soldier morale
   d. the Korean War when psychologists examined the effects of brainwashing on prisoners of War

3. A teacher who went to a restaurant for dinner did not recognize her waiter as one of her students. This phenomenon illustrates
   a. people react differently in a situation
   b. the importance of cognition
   c. the influence of the situation on our expectations
   d. how little people pay attention

4. In comparison to the sociologist, the social psychologist
   a. is more likely to study the social causes of behavior
   b. is more likely to study individuals than groups
   c. gives less attention to our internal functioning
   d. relies more heavily on correlational research

5. In comparison to personality psychology, social psychology
   a. is more concerned with the biological causes of behavior
   b. is more likely to use case studies in theory development
   c. has greater concern for how individuals usually respond
   d. has greater concern for how individuals respond differently

6. Compared to social psychology, biology
   a. is more concerned with nurture than with nature
   b. predisposes us to behave in ways that helped our ancestors survive
   c. has no interest in topics such as dating and hating
   d. can examine only simple behaviours such as stress and blood pressure

7. According to the text, which word best describes the relationship between different disciplines that study behavior?
   a. supplementary
   b. contradictory
   c. complementary
   d. competing

8. The text states that as a scientific discipline, social psychology
   a. is superior to those disciplines which assume a more subjective approach to the study of human nature
   b. can assist in explaining the meaning of life
   c. is one perspective from which we can view and better understand human nature
   d. offers explanations for human nature that often contradict the claims of other disciplines

9. Who of the following is most likely to study how religious attitudes develop within the typical individual?
   a. a sociologist
   b. a social worker
   c. a social psychologist
   d. a theologian

10. Who of the following would be most likely to study how the political attitudes of middle-class people differ from those of lower-class people?
    a. a personality psychologist
    b. a social psychologist
    c. a social biologist
    d. a sociologist

11. How prior opinions control interpretations is illustrated by
    a. Hastorf and Cantril's study of reactions to a football game
    b. Fischoff's study of the "I-Knew-It-All-Along" phenomenon
    c. Moscovici's study of social representations
    d. Bachman and O'Malley's study of the relationship between self-esteem and achievement

12. Widely held ideas and values that we take for granted and that help us make sense of our world are called
    a.   pluralistic assumptions
    b.   cultural traditions
    c.   social heuristics
    d.   social representations

13. The author of the text suggests that adjectives such as "self-actualized," "mature," and "well-   adjusted" demonstrate
    a.   how psychological concepts have hidden values
    b.   how psychological concepts are individualistic
    c.   an inordinate concern with mental health
    d.   how personality psychologists are more influential than social psychologists

14. According to the text, the fact that human thinking always involves interpretation
    a.   provides a valid reason for dismissing science
    b.   is precisely why we need scientific analysis
    c.   is a reason for preferring experimental over correlational research
    d.   has been more frequently recognized by those in the sciences than by those in the humanities

15. The naturalistic fallacy provides an example of
    a.   the hindsight bias
    b.   how values penetrate the work of the scientist
    c.   how common sense notions are often wrong
    d.   how naturalistic observation is unable to answer questions about cause-effect relationships

16. A researcher finds that Canadians bathe the average of once a day. He concludes that an educational program is necessary to encourage more frequent bathing by those who bathe less than once a day. The researcher is probably guilty of
    a.   hindsight bias
    b.   the "I-Knew-It-All-Along" phenomenon
    c.   illusory correlation
    d.   the naturalistic fallacy

17. According to the text, _____ tends to make people overconfident about the validity of their judgments and predictions.
    a.   the common sense error
    b.   the I-Knew-That phenomenon
    c.   the naturalistic fallacy
    d.   the hindsight bias

18. Which of the following is an example of hindsight bias?
    a. Predicting that John and Sally would make a good match because they are so much alike.
    b. After discovering that John and Sally are dating, saying that you could have predicted it because they are so much alike.
    c. Behind John and Sally's back, you predict the relationship will never last because they are too much alike.
    d. After discovering that John and Sally are dating, you are surprised that they like each other.

19. Hypotheses allow researchers to
    a. test the theories on which they are based
    b. give direction to research
    c. both a and b
    d. neither a nor b

20. Hypotheses are best characterized as
    a. axioms
    b. principles
    c. predictions
    d. conclusions

21. Most social-psychological research is conducted either in the field or in the
    _____ and is either correlational or _____.
    a. clinic; survey
    b. laboratory; experimental
    c. laboratory; survey
    d. clinic; experimental

22. The great strength of _____ is that it tends to occur in real-world settings   where it can examine questions regarding important factors like race, sex, and social status.
    a. correlational research
    b. field experimentation
    c. laboratory experimentation
    d. quasi-experimentation

23. Which of the following distinguishes the correlational method from experimentation?
    a. the correlational method uses a smaller group of subjects
    b. the correlational method enables researchers to study social attitudes
    c. no attempt is made to systematically manipulate one or more factors with the correlational method
    d. the findings from the correlational method are more likely to be contaminated by the experimenter's values

24. A negative correlation between degree of wealth and the likelihood of being involved in criminal activity would indicate that
    a. poverty makes people more likely to commit a crime
    b. the poor are more likely to be involved in criminal activity than are the wealthy
    c. being involved in criminal activity usually prevents people from accumulating wealth
    d. all of the above are necessarily true

25. Survey researchers obtain a representative group
    a. through random assignment
    b. by selecting at least 2000 respondents to be interviewed
    c. by taking a random sample
    d. either through telephone books or automobile registrations

26. The telephone company wants to survey its 100,000 customers. Four proposals for sampling the customers are being considered. Which would you recommend?
    a. interview every 75th person listed in the telephone directory
    b. mail a questionnaire to all 100,000 customers and assume at least 1200 will respond
    c. interview the people in every 50th residence from a postal listing of all addresses
    d. interview those 1000 persons with the highest phone bills

27. What the experimenter manipulates is called the _____ variable and the variable being measured is called the _____ variable.
    a. dependent; independent
    b. control; experimental
    c. independent; dependent
    d. experimental; control

28. In an experimental study of the effects of failure on self-esteem, self-esteem would be the
    a. control condition
    b. independent variable
    c. dependent variable
    d. experimental condition

29. A research psychologist manipulates the level of fear in human subjects in the laboratory and then examines what effect the different levels of fear have on the subjects' reaction times. In this study, reaction time is the _____ variable and the level of fear is the _____ variable.
    a. dependent; independent
    b. correlational; experimental
    c. independent; dependent
    d. experimental; correlational

30. "Random assignment" means that each person taking part in an experiment must
    a. have an equal chance of being in a given condition in the experiment
    b. be assigned to all the conditions of the experimental treatment
    c. be randomly selected from the larger population
    d. be given random responses to the experimenter's questions

31. Random assignment is necessary to
    a. insure mundane realism
    b. insure informed consent
    c. rule out pre-existing differences between subjects in different experimental conditions
    d. avoid the naturalistic fallacy

32. In a research study investigating the effects of stress on the desire to affiliate, half of the participants complete an easy test of mental ability and half complete a difficult test. What technique should the investigators use to ensure that any posttest differences in the group's desire to affiliate actually result from the differences in test difficulty?
    a. random sampling
    b. random assignment
    c. replication
    d. correlational measurement

33. You would like to know the relationship between the number of psychology courses people take and their interpersonal sensitivity. You survey college students to determine how much psychology they have taken and then have them complete a test of social sensitivity. Finally you plot the relationship. This is an example of
    a. a laboratory experiment
    b. a field experiment
    c. a correlational study
    d. participant observation

34. You want to research how helpful people are to someone who is lost. Which type of research would be best to use?
    a. laboratory research
    b. field research
    c. correlational research
    d. survey research

35. Which of the following techniques would be the most effective way of investigating the relationship between the political preferences and the age of Canadian citizens?
    a. an experiment
    b. a case study
    c. a correlational study
    d. participant observation

36. To determine whether changing one variable (like education) will produce changes in another (like income), we need to conduct _____ research.
    a. survey
    b. correlational
    c. experimental
    d. statistical

37. Which of the following research methods would be most effective in demonstrating that the presence of others improves our performance of a task?
    a. an experiment
    b. correlational study
    c. a survey
    d. a field study

38. An experiment has mundane realism if
    a. the experimental task is similar to tasks in everyday life
    b. it involves and absorbs people
    c. it is conducted in the field
    d. the experimenter deceives subjects

39. Which of the following is false according to the text?
    a. experimenters standardize their instructions to subjects to minimize demand characteristics
    b. the Canadian Psychological Association has developed a number of ethical principles to guide investigators
    c. informed consent is an important ethical principle to be followed in conducting research
    d. deception should never be used in conducting research

40. In conducting a study of conformity, the experimenters decide to tape-record the instructions that are to be presented to all subjects. Their decision is most likely an attempt to minimize the effect of
    a. hindsight bias
    b. mundane realism
    c. naturalistic fallacy
    d. demand characteristics

SHORT ESSAY QUESTIONS

Answer the following questions in the space provided.

1. What do social psychologists focus on in their research?

2. Briefly describe how social psychology differs from sociology and from personality psychology.

3. Briefly describe three ways in which the personal values of social psychologists penetrate their work.

4. Why is it important that social psychologists from around the world share information and ideas?

5. What is the "I-Knew-It-All-Along" phenomenon? What are its implications for social psychology?

6. Describe two important functions of a theory.

7. Describe the differences between a correlational study and an experimental study.

8. Explain how survey results can be biased.

9. What ethical problems do social psychologists encounter in conducting research? How have these problems been addressed?

ANSWER KEY

Chapter Review

1. scientific
   influence
   young
   century

2. situation
   person
   cognition
   social psychology

3. groups
   individuals
   experimental

4. differences
   most

5. neurobiology
   social

6. levels
   complement

7. values
   choice

8. objective
   preconceptions
   values
   naturalistic

9. hindsight
   common sense

10. theories
    predict

11. laboratory
    field
    correlational
    experimental

12. real-world
    manipulated
    cause
    effect

13. random sample
    1200
    unrepresentative
    wording
    response

14. control
    random
    ethical

Matching Terms

1. j
2. c
3. m
4. a
5. h
6. b
7. k
8. i
9. e
10. g
11. d
12. f
13. l

True-False Review

1. F	14. T
2. F	15. F
3. F	16. T
4. T	17. T
5. T	18. T
6. T	19. T
7. F	20. T
8. F	21. T
9. T	22. F
10. T	23. T
11. F	24. F
12. F	25. T
13. F	

Multiple-Choice Practice Test

1. c	21. b
2. c	22. a
3. c	23. c
4. b	24. b
5. c	25. c
6. b	26. a
7. c	27. c
8. c	28. c
9. c	29. a
10. d	30. a
11. a	31. c
12. d	32. b
13. a	33. c
14. b	34. b
15. b	35. c
16. d	36. c
17. d	37. a
18. b	38. a
19. c	39. d
20. c	40. d

CHAPTER 2
THE SELF IN A SOCIAL WORLD

CHAPTER OBJECTIVES

After completing your study of this chapter you should be able to:

1. Describe the nature of our self-concept and discuss how our beliefs about ourselves influence our thoughts and actions.
2. Describe the factors that shape our self-concept.
3. Discuss research findings regarding the accuracy of our self-knowledge.
4. Define self-efficacy and explain its relationship to behavior.
5. Give several examples of the self-serving bias and discuss why people perceive themselves in self-enhancing ways.
6. Describe how the self-serving bias can be adaptive as well as maladaptive.
7. Analyze how tactics of impression management may lead to false modesty or self-defeating behavior.

CHAPTER REVIEW

Supply the words necessary to complete each of the following statements.

SELF-CONCEPT: WHO AM I

1. Our sense of _____ helps organize our thoughts and actions. The self-_____ effect refers to the tendency to more easily remember any information that relates to one's self. The elements of our self-concept include the specific self-_____ that guide our processing of self-relevant information and the _____ selves that we dream of or dread. Our self-_____ is our overall evaluation of ourselves — how much we like or dislike ourselves.

EVALUATING OURSELVES

2. Multiple influences shape the self, including social _____ that we make when we compare ourselves to others, _____ comparisons with our past and future selves, our personal identity as well as our social _____, other people's _____ of us, and our experiences of _____ and _____.

3. We often err when _____ or _____ our behaviour and feelings. We readily _____ real influences on us and sometimes perceive factors that have little effect as _____. The subtle, _____ processes that control our behaviour may differ from our conscious, _____ explanations of it.

4. People's errors in self-understanding place limits on the scientific usefulness of their _____. Although personal testimonies are powerfully _____, they may also convey unwitting error.

5. Bandura formulated the concept of _____, that is, the sense that we are competent and effective. This sense leads us to set challenging _____ and to _____ when facing difficulties. Studies on the locus of_____ indicate that people who are self-determined are more likely to achieve and cope better than those who have a pessimistic sense of learned _____.

SELF-SERVING BIAS

6. When perceiving ourselves we are prone to a potent error: the _____ bias. This results in a tendency to blame the _____ for our failures but to accept _____ for our successes. The error is also evident in our tendency to see ourselves as generally "_____ than _____."

7. We demonstrate an unrealistic _____ about future life events. We tend to _____ the commonality of our opinions, known as false _____ and _____ the commonality of our abilities (false _____).

8. Self-serving perceptions arise partly from a motive to maintain and enhance _____, a motive that protects people from _____ but which can also contribute to misjudgment and group _____.

SELF-PRESENTATION

9. People sometimes present a different _____ than they feel. The clearest example is false _____. Sometimes people will even self-_____ with self-defeating behaviors that protect self-esteem by providing excuses for _____.

10. _____ refers to our wanting to present a desired image both to other people and to _____. Those who score high on a scale of _____ tendency adjust their behavior to create the desired impression. Those who score low are more _____ guided and more likely to say what they believe. The tendency to self-present modesty and restrained optimism is particularly great in cultures that value _____.

MATCHING TERMS

Write the letter of the correct term from the right before the appropriate number on the left.

_____ 1.   Images of whom we aspire or fear becoming.

_____ 2.   Beliefs about ourselves that influence how we perceive and remember information about us as well as others.

_____ 3.   Believing that our undesirable characteristics and behaviour are not much different than anyone else's.

_____ 4.   Protecting one's self-image by behaving in a way that creates a handy excuse for failure.

_____ 5.   Is conducive to effective coping and self-improvement.

_____ 6.   May be a by-product of how we process information or may be a result of trying to raise our self-esteem.

_____ 7.   Adjusting our social behaviour to create a favourable impression on others.

_____ 8.   The tendency to believe we are different and unique compared to others.

_____ 9.   A student who defines herself as a Chinese accounting student illustrates this aspect of her self-concept.

_____ 10. Becoming passive and depressed because one's efforts are ineffective.

_____ 11. Feeling really pleased about your performance because your test mark was the highest in the class.

_____ 12. An example of this phenomenon is assuming that I am being talked about because I overhear someone say my name.

a.   self-efficacy

b.   social comparison

c.   self-serving bias

d.   possible selves

e.   self-schema

f.   social identity

g.   false consensus effect

h.   learned helplessness

i.   self-monitoring

j.   self-handicapping

k.   false uniqueness effect

l.   self-reference effect

TRUE-FALSE REVIEW

Circle T if the statement is true and F if it is false.

T F 1. No topic in psychology is today more researched than the self.

T F 2. The self-reference effect illustrates how our sense of self is at the center of our worlds.

T F 3. Our "possible selves" include images of the self we fear becoming as well as images of the self we dream of becoming.

T F 4. A person with low self-esteem will often view his recent past self more positively than his distant past self.

T F 5. The more that students at English universities identify themselves as British the less they identify themselves as European.

T F 6. People who took a pill that they thought would produce physical arousal tolerated much more shock than people not given a pill.

T F 7. People are clearly aware of the factors that influence their daily moods.

T F 8. People are much better at predicting their own future behavior than that of others.

T F 9. Suffering a paralyzing accident affects long-term happiness less than most people suppose.

T F 10. Studies of perception and memory show that we are more aware of the <u>results</u> of thinking rather than the <u>process</u>.

T F 11. People's expressed attitudes are more likely to predict their behavior if they are first asked to analyze their feelings before indicating their attitudes.

T F 12. "Self-efficacy" is equivalent to "self-esteem."

T F 13. People with a strong sense of self-efficacy cope better and achieve more than do people who lack a sense of their own competence and effectiveness.

T F 14. People with a strong sense of internal control believe that their destiny is controlled by other people.

T F 15. Learned helplessness is likely to promote the health and happiness of a nursing home resident.

T F 16. Research indicates that those who exhibit the self-serving bias invariably have low self-esteem.

T F 17. On nearly any dimension that is both subjective and socially desirable most people see themselves as better than average.

T F 18. The better-than-average phenomenon is cited as an example of the fundamental attribution error.

T F 19. If we hold negative ideas about another racial group, we presume that many others also have negative stereotypes.

T F 20. We tend to think attractive people have personalities quite different from our own.

T F 21. The more physiologically aroused people are after a failure, the more likely they are to excuse the failure with self-protective attributions.

T F 22. People with high self-esteem are more likely to be obnoxious and interrupt others compared to those with low self-esteem.

T F 23. Mildly depressed people generally see themselves as other people see them.

T F 24. Self-handicapping is typically motivated by feelings of inferiority.

T F 25. The self-serving bias seems to be restricted to people who live in North America and Europe.

MULTIPLE-CHOICE PRACTICE TEST

Circle the correct letter.

1. Perceiving ourselves as athletic, overweight, smart, or shy constitutes our
   a. egocentric beliefs
   b. interdependent self
   c. self-schemas
   d. self-references

2. The tendency to process efficiently and remember well information related to oneself is called the _____ effect.
   a. self-aggrandizing
   b. self-schematizing
   c. self-processing
   d. self-reference

3. The spotlight effect is illustrated when we
   a. exaggerate how important an event is to us
   b. overestimate how often others notice our behaviour
   c. think we are less important to others
   d. overestimate how often people have undesirable behaviour similar to what we have

4. According to Hazel Markus and her colleagues, our "possible selves"
   a. include our vision of the self we dream of becoming and the self we fear becoming
   b. include only our vision of the self we hope we will become
   c. are the specific self-schemas that determine our self-esteem
   d. are the ideal images that close friends and relatives have of us

5. Self-esteem refers to
   a. the sum total of our possible selves
   b. our overall evaluation of ourselves
   c. the sum total of all our thoughts about ourselves
   d. our most central self-schemas

6. The fact that students tend to have a higher academic self-concept if they attend a school with few exceptionally capable students is best explained in terms of
   a. locus of control
   b. self-handicapping
   c. social comparison
   d. self-monitoring

7. A self-enhancing strategy in which we perceive our recent behaviour more positively than our more distant past behaviour is called
    a. the illusion of transparency
    b. temporal comparison
    c. the dual attitude system
    d. a self-serving bias

8. In completing the statement, "I am...." Michelle responds by stating that she is the youngest girl in her family, belongs to a sorority, and is a member of the community orchestra. Michelle's statements most clearly reflect
    a. her possible selves
    b. her social identity
    c. her personal identity
    d. a strong self-monitoring tendency

9. Charles H. Cooley's concept of the "looking-glass self" recognizes that our self-concept is shaped by
    a. the roles we play
    b. social comparison
    c. success and failure experiences
    d. other people's judgments

10. When people are asked whether they would comply with demands to deliver cruel shocks or would be hesitant to help a victim if several other people were present,
    a. they overwhelmingly deny their vulnerability to such influences
    b. they admit they might be influenced but their actual behavior is not influenced
    c. males deny they would be influenced, but females admit they would be
    d. they accurately predict their future behavior on such significant matters

11. Research has indicated that when people are asked to record their daily mood and the factors that might influence it,
    a. there is little relationship between their perception of how important a factor was and how well the factor predicted their moods
    b. females have better insight into what affects their moods than do males
    c. people have much better insight into what influences their own moods than what influences the mood of a friend
    d. adults have better insight into what affects their moods than do children

12. People's predictions about how they will feel if insulted
    a. is likely to be accurate
    b. is likely to be inaccurate
    c. is apt to involve denying that the insult will have any affect on them
    d. is apt to be very detailed

13. Timothy Wilson suggests that the mental processes that _____ our social behavior are distinct from the mental processes through which we _____ our behavior.
    a. control; explain
    b. evaluate; inhibit
    c. produce; control
    d. form; change

14. In nine experiments, Timothy Wilson and his colleagues found that people's expressed attitudes predicted their later behavior reasonably well <u>unless</u>
    a. their attitudes were inconsistent with social norms
    b. the experimenter had them under surveillance
    c. they were asked to rationally analyze their feelings before indicating their attitudes
    d. they had little opportunity to reflect on their feelings before indicating their attitudes

15. According to the text, research on self-knowledge suggests that
    a. people tend to underestimate their own abilities
    b. people with high self-esteem feel less loved than those with low self-esteem
    c. people are highly accurate in predicting their own future behaviour
    d. people's self-reports are often untrustworthy

16. Bandura is to _____ as Rotter is to _____.
    a. learned helplessness; self-serving bias
    b. interdependent self; independent self
    c. self-efficacy; locus of control
    d. self-serving bias; fundamental attribution error

17. People who believe themselves internally controlled are more likely to
    a. take unnecessary risks
    b. engage in self-handicapping
    c. be tolerant of racial differences
    d. do well in school

18. Betsy never plans ahead because she believes that the way things turn out is merely a matter of chance. Betsy's thinking most clearly illustrates
    a. the false uniqueness bias
    b. an external locus of control
    c. self-handicapping
    d. self-efficacy

19. An internal locus of control is to _____ as unrealistic optimism is to _____.
    a. self-presentation; self-serving bias
    b. self-serving bias; fundamental attribution error
    c. self-efficacy; self-serving bias
    d. self-handicapping; self-efficacy

20. Dogs who learn a sense of helplessness by being taught they cannot escape shocks
    a. tend to band together and as a group demonstrate collective efficacy
    b. tend to become highly aggressive in other situations
    c. more readily take the initiative to escape punishment when that becomes possible
    d. later fail to take the initiative in another situation when they can escape punishment

21. Because she gets poor grades no matter how hard she studies, Milly has decided not to study at all. Milly's behavior most clearly demonstrates
    a. self-serving bias
    b. unrealistic optimism
    c. learned helplessness
    d. a self-monitoring tendency

22. Judging from the discussion of self-image in the text, people are least likely to see themselves as above average in
    a. leadership ability
    b. tolerance
    c. weight
    d. helpfulness

23. Students are more likely to rate themselves as superior in _____ than in _____
    a. moral goodness; intelligence
    b. being punctual; being disciplined
    c. creativity; honesty
    d. contributing money to the poor; caring for the poor

24. College students perceive themselves as far more likely than their classmates to
_____ and as far less likely to _____.
    a. draw a good salary; develop a drinking problem
    b. obtain a divorce; own a home
    c. travel to Europe; be happy in their work
    d. become a mental patient; have close friendships

25. Unrealistic optimism, false consensus, and false uniqueness all reflect the human tendency toward
    a. self-forgetfulness
    b. self-serving bias
    c. self-efficacy
    d. self-handicapping

26. We tend to _____ the commonality of our unsuccessful behaviors and _____ the commonality of our successful behaviors.
    a. overestimate; underestimate
    b. underestimate; overestimate
    c. underestimate; underestimate
    d. overestimate; overestimate

27. Although Jeff frequently exceeds the speed limit by at least 10 miles per hour, he justifies his behavior by erroneously thinking that most other drivers do the same. His mistaken belief best illustrates
    a. learned helplessness
    b. false consensus
    c. self-monitoring
    d. false uniqueness

28. Those who evade paying income tax but who give generously to charity will probably _____ the number of others who evade taxes and _____ the number of others who give generously to charity.
    a. overestimate; overestimate
    b. underestimate; overestimate
    c. overestimate; underestimate
    d. underestimate; underestimate

29. Research on self-perception indicates that if we find ourselves linked (say born on the same day as) to some reprehensible person
    a. we show a temporary loss of self-esteem
    b. we form a more independent self
    c. we form a harsher view of the person
    d. we soften our view of the person

30. Research findings challenge the notion that
    a. most people suffer from unrealistically low self-esteem
    b. we tend to blame others for their own misfortune
    c. we strive to protect and enhance our self-esteem
    d. true humility consists of self-forgetfulness

31. Abraham Tesser has argued that a " _____ " motive is important in helping us understand friction among brothers and sisters who share similar abilities.
    a. cognitive dissonance
    b. self-esteem maintenance
    c. self-forgetfulness
    d. social approval maintenance

32. People with low self-esteem are more likely to
    a. engage in sexual activity at an inappropriately young age
    b. become dangerous when socially rejected
    c. become exceptionally aggressive
    d. become depressed and use drugs

33. High self-esteem goes hand in hand with
    a. self-serving perceptions
    b. self-monitoring
    c. an independent self
    d. a tendency to berate others

34. According to "terror management theory," positive self-esteem protects us from feeling anxiety over
    a. social rejection
    b. our own death
    c. public speaking
    d. failing to achieve an important goal

35. Those who do not exhibit self-serving bias may tend toward
    a. better than average mental health
    b. schizophrenia
    c. above average intelligence
    d. depression

36. Self-presentation and self-handicapping both reflect human efforts at
    a. self-efficacy
    b. self-understanding
    c. collective efficacy
    d. impression management

37. The self-handicapping strategy enables us to
    a. accept greater responsibility for our failures
    b. avoid the fundamental attribution error
    c. take greater credit for our successes
    d. circumvent the ill effects of the Peter Principle

38. Tomorrow morning Harry Smith has an interview which will determine whether he will be accepted into medical school. Rather than getting a good night's sleep, he is going to an all-night party with his friends. From the material presented in the text, which of the following may best describe Harry's behavior?
    a. Harry unconsciously hopes he is not accepted into medical school
    b. Harry is making the fundamental attribution error
    c. Harry is engaging in self-handicapping
    d. Harry shares with his friends a sense of collective efficacy

39. People are more modest when
    a. experts will be scrutinizing their self-evaluations
    b. they have a strong sense of self-efficacy
    c. they present themselves to others they regard as inferior
    d. they present themselves to members of their own family

40. Being attuned to the way one presents oneself in social situations and adjusting one's performance to create the desired impression is called
    a. self-handicapping
    b. self-monitoring
    c. egocentric role-playing
    d. manipulative social adjustment

SHORT ESSAY QUESTIONS

Answer the following questions in the space provided.

1. Briefly describe what is meant by our "self-schemas" and "possible selves."

2. Identify three factors that shape the development of one's self-concept.

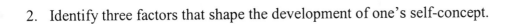

3. Discuss research findings regarding the accuracy of our self-knowledge.

4. What is self-efficacy? Briefly describe the results of research on this concept.

5. What is the self-serving bias? Describe two lines of research which demonstrate the presence of the error.

6. Explain why people perceive themselves in self-enhancing ways and briefly describe how a self-serving bias can be adaptive as well as maladaptive.

7. Explain how attempts at impression management may lead to false modesty and self-handicapping.

ANSWER KEY

Chapter Review

1. self
   reference
   schemas
   possible
   esteem

2. comparisons
   temporal
   identity
   judgments
   success
   failure

3. explaining
   predicting
   deny
   influential
   implicit
   explicit

4. self-reports
   persuasive

5. self-efficacy
   goals
   persist
   control
   helplessness

6. self-serving
   situation
   credit
   better
   average

7. optimism
   overestimate
   consensus
   underestimate
   uniqueness

8. self-esteem
   depression
   conflict

9. self
   modesty
   handicap
   failure

10. self-presentation
    ourselves
    self-monitoring
    internally
    self-restraint

Matching Terms

1. d
2. e
3. g
4. j
5. a
6. c

7. i
8. k
9. f
10. h
11. b
12. l

True-False Review

1.	T	14.	F
2.	T	15.	F
3.	T	16.	F
4.	F	17.	T
5.	T	18.	F
6.	T	19.	T
7.	F	20.	F
8.	F	21.	T
9.	T	22.	T
10.	T	23.	T
11.	F	24.	F
12.	F	25.	F
13.	T		

Multiple-Choice Practice Test

1.	c	21.	c
2.	d	22.	c
3.	b	23.	a
4.	a	24.	a
5.	b	25.	b
6.	c	26.	a
7.	b	27.	b
8.	b	28.	c
9.	d	29.	d
10.	a	30.	a
11.	a	31.	b
12.	b	32.	d
13.	a	33.	a
14.	c	34.	b
15.	d	35.	d
16.	c	36.	d
17.	d	37.	c
18.	b	38.	c
19.	c	39.	a
20.	d	40.	b

CHAPTER 3
SOCIAL BELIEFS AND JUDGMENTS

CHAPTER OBJECTIVES

After completing your study of this chapter you should be able to:
1. Discuss the assumptions, questions, and general findings of attribution theory.
2. Define the fundamental attribution error and explain why it occurs.
3. Examine how preconceptions control our interpretations and memories.
4. Explain with illustrations, the overconfidence phenomenon.
5. Describe how we use heuristics in processing information.
6. Illustrate the illusions of correlation and personal control.
7. Describe with examples, how our moods affect our judgments.
8. Describe how our erroneous beliefs may generate their own reality.

CHAPTER REVIEW

Supply the words necessary to complete each of the following statements.

EXPLAINING OTHERS

1. _____ theory analyzes how we explain people's behaviour. It suggests we explain others' behaviour either in terms of _____ or _____ causes.

2. Edward Jones and Keith Davis noted that we often infer that people's dispositions _____ to their actions. Harold Kelley described how we use information about _____, distinctiveness, and _____ in explaining behaviour. Further evidence of the reasonableness of our attributions comes from Norman Anderson's research on _____ integration.

3. The "_____ attribution error" refers to the tendency for observers to underestimate _____ influences and to overestimate _____ influences upon others' behaviour.

4. Even when people know they are _____ someone else's behaviour, they still underestimate _____ influences.

5. We commit this error when explaining _____ behaviour. We often explain our own behaviour in terms of the _____ while holding others _____ for their behaviour.

6. Why do we make this attributional error? Attribution theorists point out that we have a different _____ when observing than when acting. When we watch

6. Why do we make this attributional error? Attribution theorists point out that we have a different _____ when observing than when acting. When we watch another person act, the _____ occupies the center of our attention. When we act, the _____ commands our attention. Perspectives can change with _____ and circumstances. If people are made _____, they attribute more responsibility to themselves.

7. Other explanations have been offered for the fundamental attribution error. For example, our whole Western worldview inclines us to assume that _____ cause events. People in Eastern Asian cultures are more sensitive to the importance of _____.

8. Experiments reveal that the attribution error occurs even when we are aware of the _____ forces. The error is fundamental because it colors our _____ in basic and important ways. For example, people's attributions predict their _____ toward the poor and unemployed.

CONSTRUCTING INTERPRETATIONS AND MEMORIES

9. Certain experiments show how people's preconceptions bias the way they _____ and interpret information they are given. The effect of prior beliefs on social _____ is so great that even _____ evidence may be seen as supporting one's beliefs.

10. Studies indicate that a falsehood is difficult to demolish if people have invented an _____ for it. The belief perseverance phenomenon can be reduced by having people explain any _____ outcome. Research also indicates we easily (though unconsciously) revise our _____ to suit our knowledge. We _____ our past attitudes, past behaviour, and experiences.

JUDGING OTHERS

11. People tend to be more _____ than correct. Daniel Kahneman and Amos Tversky found that about 30 percent of the time, the correct answers lay outside the range about which people feel _____ percent confident.

12. The overconfidence phenomenon seems partly due to the fact that people are more likely to search for information that _____ their beliefs than for information that does not. Overconfidence can be reduced by giving people prompt _____ on the accuracy of their judgments and by getting them to think of one good reason why their judgments might be _____.

13. _____ are efficient thinking strategies that provide a _____ to reality. To judge something by intuitively comparing it to our mental representation of a category is to use the _____ heuristic.

14. If examples are readily _____ in our memory, we tend to assume the event is commonplace. This is called the _____ heuristic. This helps to explain why people are _____ to infer a general truth from a vivid instance but are _____ to deduce particular instances from a general truth.

15. People also tend to see _____ where none exists. They readily misperceive random events as _____ their beliefs.

16. Our tendency to perceive random events as though they were related feeds the illusion that chance events are subject to our _____. Ellen Langer demonstrated this illusion with experiments on _____. The illusion of control may arise as a result of the statistical phenomenon of _____ toward the _____.

17. Our _____ color how we recall and interpret our world. In a _____ mood, we have more depressing thoughts. When we are emotionally aroused we are more likely to make _____ judgments and to _____ others.

SELF-FULFILLING BELIEFS

18. Studies of _____ bias and teacher expectations illustrate the _____ prophecy: the tendency for our expectations to evoke behaviour that confirms them.

CONCLUSIONS

19. Our modes of thought are generally _____ and errors are a by-product of our minds' strategies for simplifying complex information.

MATCHING TERMS

Write the letter of the correct term from the right before the appropriate number on the left.

_____ 1. Throwing dice softly for low numbers and hard for high numbers.

_____ 2. Clinging to beliefs in the face of contradictory evidence.

_____ 3. Searching for information that confirms one's expectations.

_____ 4. Shows how memory is constructive.

_____ 5. The tendency for one's expectations to evoke behaviour that confirms the expectations.

_____ 6. It analyzes how we make judgments about people and explain their behaviour.

_____ 7. Perceiving order in random events.

_____ 8. Very high scorers on one exam will tend to get lower scores on the next exam.

_____ 9. Imagining alternative scenarios and outcomes that might have happened, but didn't.

_____ 10. Judging the likelihood of things by how well they match particular prototypes.

_____ 11. The tendency to overestimate the accuracy of one's beliefs.

_____ 12. The tendency for observers to underestimate situational influences and overestimate dispositional influences.

_____ 13. Judging the likelihood of events in terms of how quickly they come to mind.

a. misinformation effect

b. illusion of control

c. regression toward the average

d. counterfactual thinking

e. availability heuristic

f. overconfidence phenomenon

g. self-fulfilling prophecy

h. belief perseverance

i. illusory correlation

j. attribution theory

k. fundamental attribution error

l. representativeness heuristic

m. confirmation bias

TRUE-FALSE REVIEW

Circle T if the statement is true and F if it is false.

T F 1. Attribution theorists are primarily concerned with how we are influenced by others, particularly by groups.

T F 2. Fritz Heider concluded that people tend to attribute someone's behaviour either to stable or to unstable factors.

T F 3. If a person acts friendly we usually infer that she is a friendly person.

T F 4. Harold Kelley suggests that we use information about "correspondence" in judging the causes of another's behaviour.

T F 5. Discounting of situational effects in judging another's behaviour is called the fundamental attribution error.

T F 6. We often explain our own behaviour in terms of the situation while holding others responsible for their behaviour.

T F 7. Presuppositions clearly affect both everyday and scientific thinking.

T F 8. The Kulechov effect refers to the fact that people from Eastern cultures are less vulnerable to the fundamental attribution error.

T F 9. Memory is like a storage chest into which we deposit material. Occasionally something gets lost from the chest and then we say we have forgotten.

T F 10. Memories are often reconstructions of the past.

T F 11. Research indicates that children but not adults construct false memories.

T F 12. Much of our life is determined by unconscious mental processes.

T F 13. The more confident people are in predicting their behaviour, the more accurate they are.

T F 14. People tend to seek out confirming rather than disconfirming evidence for their beliefs.

T F 15. People are surprisingly accurate at estimating the amount of time they will need to get their work done.

T F 16. Providing people with prompt feedback on the accuracy of their judgments reduces the overconfidence phenomenon.

T F 17. Simple, efficient thinking strategies that help us simplify and cope with reality, are known as schema.

T F 18. The hindsight bias explains why people are more afraid of flying than driving.

T F 19. The availability heuristic provides an explanation for the self-fulfilling prophecy.

T F 20. People are slow to deduce particular instances from a general truth but are quick to infer general truth from a vivid instance.

T   F 21. If we miss winning the jackpot by one number we feel more frustrated than if our jackpot number was no where near the winning number.

T F 22. "Regression toward the average" may help to explain why the illusion of control arises.

T F 23. An individual who play cards against a nervous person are more likely to bet more money than when playing against a confident person.

T F 24. The results of experimenter bias demonstrate the tendency for one's expectations to evoke behaviour that confirms the expectations.

T F 25. Many published experiments have confirmed that teachers' expectations significantly influence their students' performance.

MULTIPLE-CHOICE PRACTICE TEST

Circle the correct letter.

1. Women's friendliness is especially likely to be misread as a sexual come-on by men who
    a. have no sisters
    b. are in positions of power
    c. have low self-esteem
    d. have liberal political attitudes

2. The theory of how we explain others' behaviour is known as
    a. impression theory
    b. inferential analysis theory
    c. cognitive dissonance theory
    d. attribution theory

3. According to the theory of correspondent inferences,
    a. we tend to infer that people's intentions and dispositions correspond to their actions
    b. we tend to infer that people's intentions and dispositions correspond to our own intentions and dispositions
    c. we tend to infer that people share the same underlying motives and values
    d. those who have similar values tend to make the same attributions about others

4. Evidence of the reasonable manner in which we form judgments of one another comes from research on
    a. informational influence
    b. personal space
    c. the mere-exposure effect
    d. information integration

5. According to Harold Kelley's theory of attributions, the three factors that influence whether we attribute someone's behaviour to internal or external causes are
    a. distinctiveness, consensus, relevance
    b. distinctiveness, consensus, consistency
    c. relevance, consistency, consensus
    d. distinctiveness, consistency, relevance

6. For a school debate, Sally has been asked to argue in favor of capital punishment. Research on the fundamental attribution error suggests that observers of Sally's speech will conclude that her arguments
    a. reflect her true attitude on the topic
    b. reflect a tendency to present herself favorably
    c. are weak because she was assigned to present a particular position on the topic
    d. will lead her to experience cognitive dissonance

7. The tendency for observers to underestimate the impact of the situation and overestimate the impact of inner dispositions upon another's behaviour is called
    a. the self-serving bias
    b. the false consensus bias
    c. the fundamental attribution error
    d. cognitive conceit

8. You notice that Mary has missed class and you commit the fundamental attribution error by thinking,
    a. Mary has been required to work overtime
    b. Mary is lazy
    c. Mary's friends stopped by her room unexpectedly
    d. Mary has the flu

9. When subjects were told that a clinical psychology graduate student had been instructed to act in a friendly manner or in an aloof, critical manner, they judged
    a. that the graduate student's aloof manner reflected her personality but the friendly behaviour was due to the situation
    b. both the friendly and aloof behaviours to have a situational cause
    c. that both the friendly and aloof behaviours reflected the student's true dispositions
    d. that the aloof behaviour was due to the situation but the friendly behaviour reflected her true disposition

10. According to the text, the fundamental attribution error may lead us to
    a. overestimate the brilliance of our teachers
    b. fail to hold people responsible for their misconduct
    c. be lenient with convicted criminals
    d. underestimate our own compassion

11. There is a tendency to attribute the causes of _____ behaviour to the situation and to attribute the causes of _____ behaviour to traits.
    a. our own; others'
    b. others'; our own
    c. children's; adults
    d. males'; females'

12. Our tendency to attribute others' behaviour to their personal characteristics is reduced when we
    a. view a videotape of the behaviour recorded from their perspective
    b. make judgments about criminal behaviour
    c. are high in self-efficacy
    d. make judgments about academic performance

13. People from Eastern Asian cultures are more likely than Canadians to
    a. offer situational explanations for someone's actions
    b. offer dispositional explanations for someone's actions
    c. engage in self-handicapping
    d. offer self-serving explanations for their own behaviour

14. As a result of making the fundamental attribution error you might be likely to favor
    a. increases in unemployment benefits
    b. increases in international aid to poor countries
    c. more severe penalties for criminal offenses
    d. victim compensation laws

15. Many people firmly believe in astrology's ability to predict the future. Assuming they are presented a history of an astrologer's past predictions which in actuality show a random mix of success and failure, they are likely to
    a. believe the astrologer is successful
    b. question this astrologer's predictive ability but still believe in the validity of astrology
    c. become very defensive
    d. give up their belief in the validity of astrology

16. The tendency of people to cling to their ideas even in the face of contrary evidence is called the
    a. belief perseverance phenomenon
    b. availability heuristic
    c. belief assimilation phenomenon
    d. denial paradox

17. The Kulechov effect in which people perceive different emotions in an actor's face illustrates
    a. the availability heuristic
    b. memory construction
    c. our use of useless information
    d. how preconceptions control our interpretations

18. Despite reading solid research evidence that cigarette smoking causes cancer, Philip continues to believe that smoking is harmless. Philip's thinking clearly reveals
    a. belief assimilation
    b. belief consolidation
    c. belief perseverance
    d. the operation of the availability heuristic

19. The more closely we examine our theories and explain how they might be true,
    a. the more uncertain we become of them
    b. the more closed we become to discrediting information
    c. the more open we are likely to become to discrediting information
    d. the more complex our theories are likely to become

20. The tendency of people to cling to their ideas even in the face of contrary evidence can be reduced by having them
    a. study the hindsight bias
    b. study the evidence more carefully
    c. participate in a debate
    d. explain why the opposite idea might be true

21. In recalling a scene from our past experience we often see ourselves in the scene. This illustrates how
    a. memory is a reconstruction of the past
    b. memory always involves mental imagery
    c. personal memories are often precise copies of the past
    d. memory is heuristic

22. In a study of eyewitness testimony in which students were shown a film of a traffic accident and then asked questions about what they saw, results indicated that
    a. what students recalled was shaped by the wording of the questions
    b. students' memories were precise copies of what they had seen
    c. what students recalled was a function of both their intelligence and the vividness of the film
    d. students who had themselves been involved in a similar accident viewed the film differently from students who had never been involved in an accident

23. Research indicates that participants in self-improvement programs show _____ improvement on average and claim they received _____ improvement.
    a. considerable; modest
    b. modest; considerable
    c. modest; modest
    d. considerable; considerable

24. The speed with which we process emotional stimuli, the ability of experts to recognize complex patterns, and our ability to process subliminal messages all testify to
    a. the power of the unconscious
    b. how beliefs can be self-fulfilling
    c. the reconstructive nature of memory
    d. how preconceptions shape reality

25. Although Fred was certain he answered at least 50 items correctly on his history test, he actually was right on only 40 items. Fred's misjudgment illustrates
    a. the self-fulfilling prophecy
    b. the hindsight bias
    c. the overconfidence phenomenon
    d. regression toward the average

26. When writer Chuck Ross mailed a typewritten copy of Jerzy Kosinski's previously published novel, *Steps*, to 28 publishers and literary agencies to consider for publication,
    a. he was accused of plagiarism
    b. most did not recognize it and wanted to publish it
    c. all rejected it including the original publisher
    d. all but the original publisher rejected it

27. Giving people immediate feedback on the accuracy of their judgments
    a. has successfully reduced the overconfidence bias
    b. has shown no effect on the overconfidence bias
    c. reduces overconfidence bias in children but not in adults
    d. undermines their self-confidence and leads them to make worse errors in judgment

28. Linda is 31, single, and outspoken. As a college student she was deeply concerned with discrimination and other social issues. A tendency to conclude that it is more likely that Linda is a bank teller and active in the feminist movement than simply a bank teller illustrates the powerful influence of
    a. belief perseverance
    b. the availability heuristic
    c. regression toward the average
    d. the representativeness heuristic

29. What psychological term might best be used to describe the rule "I before E except after C"?
    a. schema
    b. hindsight bias
    c. illusion of control
    d. heuristic

30. The incorrect belief that the letter "k" appears more often as the first letter of a word than as the third letter can be understood in terms of
    a. the availability heuristic
    b. hindsight bias
    c. regression toward the average
    d. the illusion of control

31. When we can imagine an alternative outcome to what has occurred, we are engaging in
    a. judgmental overconfidence
    b. illusory thinking
    c. reconstructing memories
    d. counterfactual thinking

32. People who were shown the random mix of results from a 50-day cloud-seeding experiment concluded that cloud seeding was related to the occurrence of rain. This judgment showed
    a. an illusory correlation
    b. the representativeness heuristic
    c. the misinformation effect
    d. counterfactual thinking

33. A person enters a casino and after inserting one silver dollar in a slot machine hits the jackpot. This person's tendency to continue putting money into the machine so that finally the amount lost exceeds the original winnings can perhaps best be explained in terms of
    a. self-fulfilling prophecy
    b. regression toward the average
    c. illusion of control
    d. hindsight bias

34. Tversky and Kahneman have identified _____ as a possible cause of the illusion of control.
    a. schema
    b. base-rate fallacy
    c. self-fulfilling prophecy
    d. regression toward the average

35. Bob, a baseball player, makes five hits while Joe, a member of the same team, makes none in a particular game. In the next game both obtain one hit. What term used in the text explains Bob's fewer hits and Joe's increase?
    a. overconfidence bias
    b. heuristics
    c. regression to the average
    d. schema

36. After a 1990 football game between Alabama and Auburn, victorious Alabama fans viewed _____ than did the losing Auburn fans.
    a. war as more likely and advantageous to the United States
    b. war as less likely and potentially devastating
    c. a college degree as less necessary and enriching
    d. a college degree as more valuable and enriching

37. The people in a small town become convinced that the bank where they have their savings accounts is unsound. The next day most of them demand their savings. By the end of the day the bank is unable to pay off all those who want their deposits. This is an example of
    a. regression toward the average
    b. self-fulfilling prophecy
    c. the hindsight bias
    d. illusory correlation

38. Studies of experimenter bias and teacher expectations have revealed the presence of
    a. hindsight bias
    b. illusory correlation
    c. self-fulfilling prophecy
    d. a fundamental attribution error

39. The textbook illustrates that when people speak more warmly, it is sometimes the result of
    a. the representativeness heuristic
    b. the availability heuristic
    c. the overconfidence phenomenon
    d. self-fulfilling prophecy

40. Nisbett and Ross believe that education could reduce our vulnerability to errors in social thinking and should include
    a. teaching useful slogans such as "It's an empirical question"
    b. teaching that is illustrated with vivid anecdotes and examples
    c. statistics courses that are geared to everyday problems of logic
    d. all of the above

SHORT ESSAY QUESTIONS

Answer the following questions in the space provided.

1. Briefly describe the central concern of attribution theory. According to Fritz Heider, to what two kinds of causes do we attribute behaviour?

2. What is the fundamental attribution error? Why does it occur?

3. Describe what is meant by the term "memory construction."

4. Explain why we are overconfident and how we can remedy this overconfidence.

5. Explain, with examples, what are the representativeness and the availability heuristics.

6. Provide one example of illusory correlation and one example of the illusion of control.

7. Discuss the implications of self-fulfilling prophecy for the classroom.

ANSWER KEY

Chapter Review

1. Attribution
   internal
   external

2. correspond
   consistency
   consensus
   information

3. fundamental
   situational
   dispositional

4. causing
   external

5. others'
   situation
   responsible

6. perspective
   person
   environment
   time
   self-aware

7. people
   situations

8. situational
   explanations
   attitudes

9. perceive
   perception
   contradictory

10. explanation

    alternative
    memories
    reconstruct

11. confident
    98

12. confirms
    feedback
    wrong

13. representativeness
    Heuristics
    guide

14. available
    availability
    quick
    slow

15. correlation
    confirming

16. influence
    gambling
    regression
    average

17. moods
    bad
    snap
    stereotype

18. experimenter
    self-fulfilling

19. adaptive

Matching Terms

1. b
2. h
3. m
4. a
5. g
6. j
7. i

8. c
9. d
10. l
11. f
12. k
13. e

True-False Review

1.	F	14.	T
2.	F	15.	F
3.	T	16.	T
4.	F	17.	F
5.	T	18.	F
6.	T	19.	F
7.	T	20.	T
8.	F	21.	T
9.	F	22.	T
10.	T	23.	T
11.	F	24.	T
12.	T	25.	F
13.	F		

Multiple-Choice Practice Test

1.	b	21.	a
2.	d	22.	a
3.	a	23.	b
4.	d	24.	a
5.	b	25.	c
6.	a	26.	c
7.	c	27.	a
8.	b	28.	d
9.	c	29.	d
10.	a	30.	a
11.	a	31.	d
12.	a	32.	a
13.	a	33.	c
14.	c	34.	d
15.	a	35.	c
16.	a	36.	b
17.	d	37.	b
18.	c	38.	c
19.	b	39.	d
20.	d	40.	d

CHAPTER 4
BEHAVIOUR AND ATTITUDES

CHAPTER OBJECTIVES

After completing your study of this chapter you should be able to:
1. Identify the components of an attitude.
2. Describe research findings on the relationship between attitudes and behaviour.
3. Explain the conditions under which attitudes predict behaviour.
4. Provide evidence that behaviour determines attitudes.
5. Give three explanations for why our actions affect our attitudes.
6. Describe how rewards influence attitudes.

CHAPTER REVIEW

Supply the words necessary to complete each of the following statements.

1. An attitude is a favorable or unfavorable _____ reaction toward something or someone, exhibited in one's _____, feelings, or intended _____.

DO ATTITUDES DETERMINE BEHAVIOUR?

2. During the 1960s research findings led social psychologists to question whether _____ determine _____. At about the same time personality psychologists began to suspect that personality _____ also fail to predict _____. As a result the developing picture of what controls our behaviour seemed to focus on _____ factors.

3. Social psychologists never get a direct reading on people's attitudes. Instead they measure _____ attitudes, which like other behaviours, are subject to _____ influences. Jones and Sigall invented the bogus _____, which is a procedure for detecting people's true attitudes.

4. Attitudes predict behaviour when other _____ upon our behaviour are minimized, when the attitude is specifically _____ to the observed behaviour, and when the attitude is _____. Making people _____ promotes consistency between words and deeds. Attitudes forged through _____ are more likely to guide actions.

DOES BEHAVIOUR DETERMINE ATTITUDES?

5. An important lesson recent social psychology teaches is that we are likely not only to _____ ourselves into a way of acting but also to _____ ourselves into a way of thinking.

6. For example, the actions prescribed by a social _____ readily shape a person's attitudes. People come to believe what they _____, provided they are not bribed or coerced into doing so. Research on the _____ phenomenon indicates that performing a small act (for example, agreeing to do a small favor) later makes people more willing to do a larger one.

7. _____ acts corrode one's conscience, and aggressors frequently _____ their victims. Fortunately the principle works in the other direction as well. _____ action strengthens one's conscience.

8. More positive interracial behaviour may lead to the reduction of racial _____. Brainwashing includes a gradual _____ of demands and active _____ in an attempt to change a person's loyalties.

WHY DO ACTIONS AFFECT ATTITUDES?

9. _____ theory assumes that people express attitudes in line with their _____ to create a good impression.

10. Cognitive _____ theory states that people are motivated to justify their behaviour after acting contrary to their attitudes or after making a difficult _____. The theory further proposes that the less _____ justification we have for an undesirable action, the more we will feel _____ for it and thus the more _____ is aroused and the more our attitudes change.

11. _____ theory assumes that when we are _____ of our attitudes we simply observe our _____ and its circumstances and infer what our attitudes must be. An important implication of this theory is the _____ effect: rewarding people to do what they like doing anyway turns their pleasure into work.

12. Dissonance theory explains attitude _____ while self-perception theory explains attitude _____.

MATCHING TERMS

Write the letter of the correct term from the right before the appropriate number on the left.

_____ 1.   Appearing moral without being so.

_____ 2.   The tendency for people who have first agreed to a small request to comply later with a larger request.

_____ 3.   A consequence of bribing people to do what they already like doing.

_____ 4.   Actions expected of those who occupy a particular social position.

_____ 5.   Includes beliefs, feelings, and behaviour tendencies.

_____ 6.   Reduction of dissonance by internally justifying one's behaviour when external inducements do not fully justify it.

_____ 7.   Uses the principle of active participation to shape thought.

_____ 8.   Presumably uses miniature muscular responses to measure attitudes.

_____ 9.   A technique for getting people to agree to do something.

_____ 10. Expressing oneself and behaving in ways designed to create a favorable impression or an impression that corresponds to one's ideals.

_____ 11. When we are unsure of our attitudes we infer them by examining our behaviour.

_____ 12. Tension which results when two beliefs are inconsistent.

a.   attitude

b.   bogus pipeline

c.   foot-in-the-door phenomenon

d.   low-ball technique

e.   cognitive dissonance

f.   self-presentation theory

g.   insufficient justification effect

h.   self-perception theory

i.   overjustification effect

j.   brainwashing

k.   moral hypocrisy

l.   role

TRUE-FALSE REVIEW

Circle T if the statement is true and F if it is false.

T F 1. An attitude is composed of beliefs, feelings, and inclinations to act.

T F 2. Allan Wicker reported that the expressed attitudes of a group of people predict about 90 percent of the variations in their behaviours.

T F 3. The bogus pipeline is a brainwashing technique.

T F 4. People's expressed religious attitudes show no relationship to the total quantity of their religious behaviours over a period of time.

T F 5. Attitudes toward contraception strongly predict contraceptive use.

T F 6. People's expressed attitudes predict their average behaviour much better than their behaviour in a specific situation.

T F 7. People who are made self-conscious by looking into a mirror act more in line with their attitudes.

T F 8. Acting like a successful student will not make you believe you are a successful student.

T F 9. Research indicates that if people have granted a small request they are more likely to refuse to grant a larger request that comes later.

T F 10. "Low-balling" is an example of the overjustification effect.

T F 11. The low-ball technique has proven to be ineffective because it assumes attitudes determine behaviour.

T F 12. Appeals for safe driving habits have had less effect on accident rates than have lower speed limits and divided highways.

T F 13. Experiments indicate that positive behaviour toward someone fosters liking for that person.

T F 14. Severe threats tend to be more effective than mild threats in getting children to internalize a moral principle.

T F 15. Research would suggest that to change racist behaviour one must first change racist attitudes.

T F 16. A gradual escalation of demands and active participation are both components of effective brainwashing.

T F 17. "Self-presentation" involves not just impressing others but expressing our ideals and identity.

T F 18. People will adopt attitudes, which they don't believe in, in order to make a favourable impression on others.

T F 19. Dissonance is likely to occur after making an important and difficult decision.

T F 20. Dissonance theory predicts that when there is external justification for performing an act, dissonance will be high.

T F 21. Voters indicate more confidence in their candidate just after voting than just before voting.

T F 22. Self-perception theory assumes that we infer our own attitudes by looking at our behaviour.

T F 23. The greater the reward promised for an activity, the more one will come to enjoy the activity.

T F 24. Cognitive dissonance theory provides a better explanation for the overjustification effect than does self-perception theory.

T F 25. Research indicates that alcohol can provide a substitute way to reduce dissonance.

MULTIPLE-CHOICE PRACTICE TEST

Circle the correct letter.

1. The "ABCs of attitudes" refers to
    a. aptitudes, brainwashing, and cognition
    b. attraction, behaviour, and compliance
    c. affect, behaviour, and cognition
    d. affect, bogus pipeline, and cognitive dissonance

2. Which of the following is a component of Mary's attitude toward smoking?
    a. Mary believes smoking is harmful to one's health
    b. Mary dislikes the fact that people are permitted to smoke in vehicles of public transportation
    c. Mary is actively working for legislation which would outlaw the sale of cigarettes
    d. all of the above are part of Mary's attitude toward smoking

3. In 1971 social psychologist Allan Wicker said, "It may be desirable to abandon the attitude concept." Wicker made this statement because
    a. no one could provide an adequate measure of attitudes
    b. attitudes did not seem to have much effect on behaviour
    c. social psychologists could not agree on a definition of an attitude
    a. the study of attitudes had obscured the study of other influences on behaviour

4. Which of the following is a technique for measuring attitudes?
    a. self-monitoring pipeline
    b. foot-in-the-door phenomenon
    c. low-ball technique
    d. bogus pipeline

5. Based on recent social-psychological research, which of the following statements is true?
    a. our attitudes and our behaviour are unrelated
    b. our attitudes determine our behaviour but our behaviour does not determine our attitudes
    c. our behaviour determines our attitudes but our attitudes do not determine our behaviour
    d. under certain circumstances attitudes do predict behaviour

6. Joe doesn't have a very positive attitude toward women. While out walking, he sees a lady in front of him drop her groceries on the ground. A social psychologist would predict that
   a. Joe would probably help the lady pick up her groceries
   b. Joe would never help the lady
   c. Joe would laugh at the lady and her spilled groceries
   d. there is no way to predict Joe's behaviour in this specific situation

7. Research suggests that to change health habits through persuasion, we should alter people's attitudes toward
   a. specific health practices
   b. the general concept of "health fitness"
   c. health authorities
   d. the value of life itself

8. Regan and Fazio found that while all university students expressed a negative attitude toward a housing shortage which had some students sleeping in the dormitory lounges, only _____ acted on their attitudes, for example signing a petition.
   a. self-monitoring students
   b. those with mirrors in their rooms
   c. those whose attitudes arose from direct experience with the temporary housing
   d. those who were former members of a radical social movement

9. According to the text, our attitudes will predict our behaviour if
   a. we are made aware of social norms
   b. the attitudes are unrelated to central values
   c. as we act, we are conscious of our attitudes
   d. we feel anxious or insecure

10. When a movie version was made of William Golding's novel Lord of the Flies,
   a. the youngsters who acted it out became the creatures prescribed by their roles
   b. hypnosis was used to get the youngsters to live in their roles
   c. action therapy was necessary to get the youngsters to unlearn their roles
   d. the foot-in-the-door phenomenon led the youngsters who acted it out to become uncivilized and brutal

11. Researchers found that after complying with a request to display a 7.5 centimetre "Be a safe driver" sign, people were
    a. more likely to obey traffic laws
    b. more likely to break the speed limit
    c. less likely to comply later with a request to place a large, ugly "Drive Carefully" sign in their front yards
    d. more likely to comply later with a request to place a large, ugly "Drive Carefully" sign in their front yards

12. A car salesman offers to sell a customer a new car for $17,000 which is a very attractive price. After the customer signs the papers to purchase at that price, the salesman seeks final approval from the manager. He returns to tell the customer that the manager will sell the car for $17,700. The customer still agrees to buy. The customer was a victim of
    a. the overjustification effect
    b. low-balling
    c. brainwashing
    d. the door-in-the-face phenomenon

13. To prevent customers from canceling their purchases, encyclopedia salespeople may
    a. have the customer fill out the sales agreement
    b. make a second call to the customer three days after the sale
    c. attempt to sell a second more expensive item to the customer
    d. recruit the customer to be an encyclopedia salesperson

14. The tendency for oppressors to disparage their victims is given in the text as an example of
    a. how attitudes determine behaviour
    b. how behaviour determines attitudes
    c. the low-balling effect
    d. how role playing comes to shape one's self-identity

15. John, a bully, enjoys tormenting kids who are younger and weaker than he is. John will probably
    a. believe his victims deserve what they get
    b. feel guilty about his behaviour
    c. feel he should be a better person
    d. think his behaviour is acceptable because society accepts violence as a way of life

16. Which of the following is cited in the text as an example of how changing behaviour can alter attitudes?
    a. liquor laws
    b. prohibition
    c. traffic laws
    d. capital punishment legislation

17. When severe and mild threats were used in an attempt to prevent children from engaging in a prohibited activity,
    a. only the severe threat was strong enough to deter the children from engaging in the prohibited activity
    b. both threats deterred the children, but those given the mild threat showed greater internalization of the rule
    c. both threats deterred the children, but those given the severe threat showed greater internalization of the rule
    d. neither threat was successful in getting the children to internalize the rule

18. The gradual escalation of demands and active participation were described as key elements in
    a. the overjustification effect
    b. brainwashing
    c. the underjustification effect
    d. the low-balling effect

19. Which of the following is not given in the text as an example of how behaviour shapes attitudes?
    a. brainwashing of American POWs
    b. children's resistance to temptation
    c. the German greeting of "Heil Hitler"
    d. the bogus-pipeline effect

20. Which of the following theories suggests that people express attitudes in line with how they acted in order to avoid looking foolishly inconsistent?
    a. cognitive dissonance theory
    b. self-perception theory
    c. self-presentation theory
    d. role-playing theory

21. In unfamiliar social situations Philip always sizes up his audience before stating an opinion. He only makes statements he knows others will support. Philip would probably obtain a high score on a scale of
    a. self-monitoring
    b. low-balling
    c. internal control
    d. social comparison

22. The author of cognitive dissonance theory was
    a. Wicker
    b. Bem
    c. Festinger
    d. Bandura

23. According to the text, we are least likely to feel dissonance when we
    a. have made a difficult decision
    b. do not feel responsible for our behaviour
    c. have harmed a friend
    d. have been paid a small sum of money for telling a lie

24. Although John is strongly opposed to stricter parking regulations on campus, he is asked to write a paper supporting them. Dissonance theory predicts that his attitude will undergo the most change if he
    a. refuses to write the paper
    b. agrees to write the paper for $200
    c. agrees to write the paper for no pay
    d. refuses to write the paper even after being offered $20

25. In which of the following situations would cognitive dissonance theorists predict that the person is experiencing dissonance?
    a. Dan is trying to decide whether to buy a new or used bicycle
    b. just as Mike finishes mowing the lawn, it begins to rain
    c. Sara has just been accepted into law school
    d. Nancy has just chosen to attend City College rather than State University after receiving equally attractive scholarship offers from both

26. Research has indicated that racetrack bettors who have just placed their bets
    a. are more optimistic about their bet than those who are about to bet
    b. are less confident about their bet than those who are about to bet
    c. are less enthusiastic about the sport of horse racing than those who are about to bet
    d. are more susceptible to persuasive attempts than those who are about to bet

27. Both cognitive dissonance theory and self-perception theory provide an explanation for
    a. the hindsight bias
    b. the insufficient justification effect
    c. the overjustification effect
    d. moral hypocrisy

28. The theory that states we adopt certain attitudes in order to justify our past actions is
    _____ theory.
    a. cognitive dissonance
    b. self-presentation
    c. self-perception
    d. psychological reactance

29. "Let me see, do I like Chinese food? I guess I do because I eat at a Chinese restaurant twice a month." The process reflected in this internal dialogue is best understood in terms of
    a. cognitive dissonance theory
    b. self-perception theory
    c. reinforcement theory
    d. equity theory

30. According to self-perception theory, behaviour shapes attitudes
    a. only of self-monitoring people
    b. when behaviour is inconsistent with attitudes
    c. when attitudes are weak and ambiguous
    d. only in the area of politics and religion

31. College students experienced more empathy for a victim receiving electric shock when they were told
    a. something about the victim's life history
    b. that the victim would later be compensated for receiving the shock
    c. that the victim would later reverse roles with the person delivering the shock
    d. to imitate the victim's expression of pain

32. Rewards and praise that inform people of their achievements _____ intrinsic motivation. Rewards that seek to control people _____ intrinsic motivation.
    a. strengthen; strengthen
    b. weaken; strengthen
    c. strengthen; weaken
    d. weaken; weaken

33. According to self-perception theory, rewards do not diminish intrinsic interest if
    a. the rewards are unanticipated
    b. the rewards are large
    c. the rewards are small
    d. social approval accompanies any monetary reward

34. The theory that best explains the overjustification effect is
    a. cognitive dissonance theory
    b. self-presentation theory
    c. self-perception theory
    d. aggregation theory

35. Nicole loses her former interest in playing the piano after her father promises to pay her two dollars for each hour of practice. This illustrates the _____ effect.
    a. insufficient justification
    b. low-ball
    c. overjustification
    d. door-in-the-face

36. According to the text which of the following is true of self-perception and cognitive dissonance theories?
    a. self-perception theory has significantly more support than cognitive dissonance theory
    b. cognitive dissonance theory has been proven correct and self-perception theory is still being tested
    c. they are contradictory theories; therefore both cannot have validity
    d. evidence exists to support both theories, suggesting wisdom in both

37. Students who had been induced to write an essay favoring a big tuition increase reduced their dissonance by adjusting their attitudes unless
    a. after writing the essay they drank alcohol
    b. they were related to the administrators at the college
    c. they were college seniors
    d. they were hypocritical persons

38. According to Claude Steele, people are aroused by their dissonant behaviour because it often
    a. leads to physical punishment
    b. challenges their sense of purpose or meaning in life
    c. threatens their sense of self-worth
    d. leads to social rejection

39. Milford has always strongly believed that it is wrong to cheat. But after he himself cheats on a chemistry quiz, his attitude toward cheating becomes significantly less harsh. What best accounts for this attitude shift?
    a. cognitive dissonance theory
    b. self-perception theory
    c. reinforcement theory
    d. role-playing theory

40. Self-perception theory is to _____ as dissonance theory is to _____.
    a. attitude formation; attitude change
    b. attitude change; attitude formation
    c. impression formation; self-monitoring
    d. self-monitoring; impression formation

SHORT ESSAY QUESTIONS

Answer the following questions in the space provided.

1. Briefly describe the major components of an attitude.

2. What research findings led social and personality psychologists in the 1960s to emphasize the importance of external social influences on behaviour?

3. Identify three conditions under which attitudes are likely to predict behaviour.

4. Discuss four lines of evidence that indicate behaviour affects attitude.

5. How does self-presentation theory explain the effect of our actions on our attitude reports?

6. Briefly compare and contrast self-perception theory and cognitive dissonance theory.

7. Explain the insufficient justification effect and the overjustification effect.

ANSWER KEY

Chapter Review

1. evaluative
    beliefs
    behaviour

2. attitudes
    behaviour
    traits
    behaviour
    external

3. expressed
    outside
    pipeline

4. influences
    relevant
    potent
    self-aware
    experience

5. think
    act

6. role
    say
    foot-in-the-door

7. Cruel
    disparage
    Moral

8. prejudice
    escalation
    participation

9. Self-presentation
    actions
    self-monitoring

10. dissonance
    decision
    external
    responsible
    dissonance

11. Self-perception
    unsure
    behaviour
    overjustification

12. change
    formation

Matching Terms

1. k
2. c
3. i
4. l
5. a
6. g

7. j
8. b
9. d
10. f
11. h
12. e

True-False Review

1. T
2. F
3. F
4. F
5. T
6. T
7. T
8. F
9. F
10. F
11. F
12. T
13. T

14. F
15. F
16. T
17. T
18. T
19. T
20. F
21. T
22. T
23. F
24. F
25. T

Multiple-Choice Practice Test

1.	c	21.	a
2.	d	22.	c
3.	b	23.	b
4.	d	24.	c
5.	d	25.	d
6.	d	26.	a
7.	a	27.	b
8.	c	28.	a
9.	c	29.	b
10.	a	30.	c
11.	d	31.	d
12.	b	32.	c
13.	a	33.	a
14.	b	34.	c
15.	a	35.	c
16.	c	36.	d
17.	b	37.	a
18.	b	38.	c
19.	d	39.	a
20.	c	40.	a

CHAPTER 5
CULTURE, LANGUAGE, AND GENDER

CHAPTER OBJECTIVES

After completing your study of this chapter you should be able to:
1. Identify two important perspectives on human similarities and differences.
2. Describe the major themes of evolutionary psychology.
3. Discuss the nature and function of norms.
4. Identify some differing cultural norms and at least one universal norm.
5. Describe the nature of roles and the various effects of role-playing.
6. Explain the differences between individualism and collectivism and their influence on the sense of self.
7. Describe the similarities and differences between holistic and analytical reasoning and their impact on thinking about and perceiving the world.
8. Describe the similarities and differences in how cultures express and experience emotions.
9. Explain how language and culture both shape and influence each another.
10. Discuss how gender roles vary with culture and over time.
11. Describe the relationship between biology and culture and discuss the "great lesson" of social psychology.

CHAPTER REVIEW

Supply the words necessary to complete each of the following statements.

HUMAN NATURE AND CULTURAL DIVERSITY
1. Social _____ has become the explosive problem of our time. Two perspectives dominate current thinking when viewing human _____ and _____. The _____ perspective emphasizes human kinship and the _____ perspective emphasizes human diversity.

2. Evolutionary psychologists study how _____ selection favors adaptive physical and psychological traits that promote the perpetuation of one's _____. The evolutionary perspective highlights our _____ human nature.

3. Among our universal similarities, the hallmark of our species is our capacity to _____ and to adapt. It enables those in one _____ to value promptness and frankness while those in another do not.

4. All cultures have their own norms, or _____ for accepted and expected behaviour. Norms restrain and control but they also _____ the social machinery so that our words and actions come effortlessly. Cultures vary in their norms for expressiveness and _____ space. North Americans prefer to have _____ space than do Latin Americans just as men keep more _____ from one another than do women.

5. Although cultural norms vary greatly, Roger Brown has described one _____ norm which concerns how people of unequal _____ relate to one another. We communicate formally and more respectfully with strangers and those of _____ status, and informally with intimates and those of _____ status. Increased _____ is usually initiated by the person with higher status.

6. A role is a set of _____ associated with a given social position. People assigned a _____ status come to see themselves as meriting favorable treatment. Likewise, playing a _____ role can have demeaning effects which undermine self-efficacy. However, role-playing can also be used constructively. Through role _____ we can develop empathy for another.

CULTURE AND THE SELF

7. Some people, especially in industrialized Western cultures, value _____ (giving priority to one's own goals) and nurture an _____ self. Others, for example in Asian and African cultures, place greater value on _____ (giving priority to the goals of one's group) and nurture an _____ self. These contrasting ideas contribute to cultural differences in social behaviour.

8. Self-esteem in collectivist cultures correlates with what _____ think of the person. In individualistic cultures, self-esteem is more _____.

CULTURE AND REASONING

9. People from Western cultures prefer _____ explanations for others' behaviour, emphasizing an _____ style of reasoning. People from Eastern cultures perceive the world more _____ and are more likely to see the _____ as a cause for behaviour. However, both Eastern and Western cultures view _____ as an important cause of behaviour.

CULTURE AND EMOTION

10. Some of our _____ and _____ mean different things in different parts of the world. However, all cultures share a common language of _____ expressions but differ in how intensely people express _____.

11. Culture shapes not only our _____ of emotion but also influences how we _____ situations.

LANGUAGE

12. According to Benjamin Lee Whorf, language shapes _____. In fact, there is evidence to suggest that _____ can even shape the way people see themselves.

13. Bilingual education in Canada has shown that immersion students develop a deeper _____ for French-Canadian culture. However learning a second language can pose serious problems for linguistic minorities if bilingualism raises the possibility that their _____ language and even their _____ may die.

GENDER

14. In all countries, women have a more _____ self, whereas men have a more _____ self. Behaviour _____ for males and females define gender roles.

15. The impact of _____ on gender roles is enormous and is evident from the striking _____ in gender roles throughout the world and across _____. Much of this influence is transmitted through _____ as well as parents.

CONCLUSIONS

16. _____ and _____ explanations need not be contradictory. What biology initiates, culture may _____. They also _____ with one another.

17. Power resides in both persons and situations. They _____ in at least three ways. First, individuals vary in how they interpret and _____ to a given situation. Second, people _____ many of the situations that influence them. Third, people help _____ their social situations.

MATCHING TERMS

Write the letter of the correct term from the right before the appropriate number on the left.

_____ 1.   Important vehicle of cultural influence.

_____ 2.   A set of behaviour expectations for males and females.

_____ 3.   Reasoning that considers all possible consequences.

_____ 4.   Natural selection and cultural selection working together.

_____ 5.   They prescribe proper behaviour.

_____ 6.   The taboo against incest.

_____ 7.   Process that results in the survival of the fittest.

_____ 8.   Self defined in relation to others.

_____ 9.   The relationship between persons and situations.

_____ 10.   A technique that can produce empathy for others.

_____ 11.   Study of how natural selection favours social behaviours that will protect one's genes.

_____ 12.   Giving priority to one's own goals rather than to group goals.

_____ 13.   A shared heritage that is passed down from generation to generation

_____ 14.   Its size depends upon our familiarity with whoever is near us.

_____ 15.   Reasoning that emphasizes rules.

a.   natural selection

b.   evolutionary psychology

c.   culture

d.   norms

e.   personal space

f.   a universal norm

g.   role reversal

h.   individualism

i.   interdependent self

j.   holistic reasoning

k.   analytical reasoning

l.   gender role

m.   peers

n.   coevolution

o.   interaction

TRUE-FALSE REVIEW

Circle T if the statement is true and F if it is false.

T F 1. An evolutionary perspective tends to emphasize our human kinship rather than our diversity.

T F 2. Among our universal similarities, the hallmark of our species is our capacity to learn and to adapt.

T F 3. Much of our behaviour is socially programmed rather than biologically programmed.

T F 4. Because we encounter so many different people daily, culture has little impact on us.

T F 5. The portable bubble that we like to maintain between ourselves and others is called a cognitive map.

T F 6. The taboo against incest is a universal norm.

T F 7. Brown's universal norm is primarily concerned with the way males and females relate to each other.

T F 8. All societies rank people by authority and status.

T F 9. A role is defined by a whole cluster of norms.

T F 10. As we internalize a role we become more self-conscious.

T F 11. Role-playing is always destructive to interpersonal relationships.

T F 12. People assigned a superior status often think they are more intelligent than lower status people.

T F 13. Japanese people are more likely than North Americans to complete the statement "I am…" by stating their personal traits or personal goals.

T F 14. Social responsibilities are more important to an individualistic culture than are personal responsibilities.

T F 15.   Collectivist cultures do not see behaviour as the result of dispositional attributions.

T F 16.   Facial expressions have different meanings in different cultures.

T F 17.   Language shapes reality.

T F 18.   The term "gender role" refers to one's feeling of being a male or female.

T F 19.   Most people present themselves to the opposite sex in ways that meet gender role expectations.

T F 20.   Male gender roles have not changed over the last century.

T F 21.   In many cultures, boys spend as much time as girls helping with housework and child care.

T F 22.   By living in one neighborhood rather than another, parents can alter the odds that their children will use drugs or get pregnant.

T F 23.   Coevolution is really just another term for role reversal.

T F 24.   The height norm (male taller norm) is the result of both evolutionary and cultural programming.

T F 25.   The great lesson of social psychology is that persons and situations interact.

MULTIPLE-CHOICE PRACTICE TEST

Circle the correct letter.

1. The cultural perspective highlights the importance of _____ in explaining the diversity of languages, customs, and expressive behaviours across the world.
   a. natural selection
   b. role playing
   c. hormonal factors
   d. human adaptability

2. The evolutionary perspective is to the cultural perspective as _____ is to _____.
   a. gender role; social role
   b. coevolution; empathy
   c. role; norm
   d. human kinship; human diversity

3. The enduring behaviours, ideas, attitudes, and traditions shared by a large group of people and transmitted from one generation to the next defines
   a. social roles
   b. coevolution
   c. ingroup bias
   d. a culture

4. The study of how natural selection predisposes adaptive traits and behaviour is called
   a. behavioural genetics
   b. biological behaviourism
   c. evolutionary psychology
   d. genetic psychology

5. According to evolutionary psychologists, which of the following is most fundamental to understanding the development of social behaviour?
   a. cultural norms
   b. hormonal factors
   c. natural selection
   d. brain organization

6. Which of the following is not an essential aspect of culture?
   a. it embodies traditions shared by a large group of people
   b. it is transmitted from one generation to the next
   c. it is a collection of behaviours that are shaped by evolutionary forces
   d. it is a set of enduring behaviours, ideas, and attitudes

7. Norms, according to the text,
    a. are composed of a set of roles
    b. prescribe proper behaviour
    c. are social behaviours of typical or average people
    d. are laws that govern the distribution of social rewards

8. Which of the following is true?
    a. there are really no truly universal norms
    b. religion does not exist in some societies
    c. norms can restrain us so subtly that we hardly sense their existence
    d. a "pedestrian" would be an example of a role

9. "Drivers are expected to keep to the right on a two-lane road" would be an example of what the text calls a
    a. norm
    b. role
    c. position
    d. status

10. Which of the following is not true about personal space?
    a. adults maintain more distance than children
    b. men keep more distance from one another than do women
    c. cultures near the equator prefer more space than cultures far from the equator
    d. there are important individual group differences in preferences for personal space

11. Who of the following maintains the least personal space?
    a. British
    b. Americans
    c. Arabs
    d. Scandinavians

12. Roger Brown's "universal norm" is
    a. the incest taboo
    b. that we relate to people of higher status the way we do to strangers
    c. that people the world over tend to relate to people of inferior status in the way they relate to strangers
    d. the prohibition of theft

13. Which of the following friendship norms seems to be universal?
    a. be prompt in keeping appointments with a friend
    b. respect the friend's privacy
    c. help the friend find a suitable spouse
    d. ask the friend's opinion before making a major decision

14. Which of the following illustrates Roger Brown's "universal norm"?
    a. brothers do not have sexual relations with their sisters in Daneria
    b. the King of Sindab invites subjects to his castle for dinner before they invite him to their huts for dinner
    c. friends in Transylvania do not divulge things said in confidence
    d. males rather than females initiate sexual relations in Wallonia

15. A social role is defined by a whole cluster of _____ that accompany a social position.
    a. schemas
    b. biases
    c. traits
    d. norms

16. Which of the following would be least likely to be considered a role?
    a. college president
    b. wife
    c. father
    d. bicyclist

17. The case of Stephen Reid illustrates
    a. the powerful effect of roles
    b. how natural selection predisposes psychological traits
    c. how role reversal promotes altruism
    d. the process of coevolution

18. Which of the following demonstrates that role-playing can be constructive?
    a. role reversal
    b. normative roles
    c. role diffusion
    d. collectivism

19. By lottery people became either managers or clerks in a simulated business office. After the managers gave orders and performed higher-level work both the managers and clerks
    a. experienced a higher sense of self-efficacy
    b. experienced burnout
    c. viewed the managers as undeserving of their role
    d. viewed the managers as more intelligent, assertive, and supportive

20. Individualism is to _____ as collectivism is to _____.
    a. North American cultures; western European cultures
    b. industrialized Western cultures; Asian cultures
    c. third world cultures; Asian cultures
    d. Mexico; Canada

21. When would a Japanese student be most likely to report positive emotions like happiness?
    a. when feeling superior to others
    b. when feeling proud of an accomplishment
    c. when a firefighter is recognized as going above and beyond her duty while fighting a house fire
    d. when feeling close to a friend

22. In comparison to people in Western cultures, people in Asian cultures are more likely to demonstrate
    a. independent self
    b. self-handicapping
    c. self-serving bias
    d. an interdependent self

23. What type of self would feel most comfortable arriving alone to study at a foreign college?
    a. an interdependent self
    b. a holistic self
    c. a collectivistic self
    d. an independent self

24. A person from a collectivist culture is more likely to experience _____ than _____.
    a. shame in group failure; pride in group achievement
    b. shame in personal failure; pride in personal achievement
    c. pride in personal achievement; shame in group failure
    d. pride in personal achievement; pride in group achievement

25. On Dec. 5, 1989, Marc Lepine shot and killed 14 female students at the University of Montreal because of his hatred against women. This explanation illustrates
    a. an emphasis on situational causes
    b. analytical reasoning
    c. holistic reasoning
    d. how collectivist culture would explain the incident

26. Which of the following emotions would be recognized the world over?
    a. gratitude
    b. disappointment
    c. surprise
    d. shame

27. According to research which of the following statements is false?
    a. bilingual students perform better on intelligence tests
    b. bilingual students are more flexible in their thinking
    c. immersion students develop less appreciation for French-Canadian culture
    d. language education can improve a student's skills

28. Research indicates that a gender difference exists in
    a. amount of household work performed
    b. fulfilling gender role expectaions
    c. problem-solving ability
    d. wanting a career

29. A set of behaviour expectations for males or females is a
    a. gender norm
    b. sex-role preference
    c. gender assignment
    d. gender role

30. In terms of the process of gender socialization, girls are to _____ as boys are to _____.
    a. legs; arms
    b. flowers; stems
    c. bread; butter
    d. roots; wings

31. Compared to college women who expected to meet a sexist male college senior, those women expecting to meet a male who presumably liked strong, ambitious women
    a. demonstrated a confused sense of gender identity
    b. performed more intelligently on a problem-solving task
    c. demonstrated stronger ethnic prejudice
    d. perceived other women as less empathic, competent, and friendly

32. Where are you most likely to find traditional gender role behaviour?
    a. Nigeria
    b. Germany
    c. Canada
    d. nomadic societies

33. Research in developmental psychology indicates that
    a. genetic influences explain about 70 percent of our individual variations in personality traits
    b. siblings are as different from one another as are pairs of children selected randomly from the population
    c. the home is the most important influence in shaping a child's personality traits
    d. children and youth learn their games, musical tastes, and even their dirty words mostly from their siblings

34. Research suggests that twelve-year-old Rafael is most likely to become a smoker if
    a. his parents smoke
    b. his friends smoke
    c. his brothers smoke
    d. his sisters smoke

35. According to the text, which of the following is true of the biological and cultural perspectives?
    a. biological and cultural factors are independent of one another
    b. biological and cultural perspectives are contradictory
    c. biological and cultural factors interact
    d. biological and cultural perspectives are actually identical

36. According to Alice Eagly, biology and culture contribute to sex differences in behaviour
    a. by influencing the roles people play
    b. by directly determining the personal traits of males and females
    c. through the process of natural selection
    d. by influencing the verbal and nonverbal communication styles of males and females

37. In essentially every known society,
    a. men are socially dominant
    b. women are more aggressive
    c. there are more male than female physicians
    d. males are responsible for finding enough food to eat

38. Which of the following is true of the relationship between persons and situations?
    a. a given situation affects different people differently
    b. people choose many of their situations
    c. people help create the situations that affect them
    d. all of the above are true

39. The way that evolutionary psychology explains behaviour could be criticized as suggestive of
    a. the base-rate fallacy
    b. counterfactual thinking
    c. hindsight bias
    d. regression toward the average

40. Which of the following statements is true?
    a. humans are more alike than different
    b. we live as homogeneous ethnic groups in separate regions
    c. second language learning poses problems for linguistic minorities
    d. we create and are created by our social worlds

SHORT ESSAY QUESTIONS

Answer the following questions in the space provided.

1. Contrast the evolutionary and cultural perspectives on human similarities and differences.

2. Define a "norm" and give one specific example of how norms vary by culture.

3. Describe Roger Brown's universal norm.

4. Define the concept of "role" and discuss the positive and negative effects of role-playing.

5. Explain how Western and Eastern cultures differ in their shaping of the self.

6. Discuss the similarities and differences in holistic and analytical reasoning in explaining behaviour.

7. Describe how gender roles vary with culture and over time.

8. What conclusion does the text reach regarding the relationship between biological and cultural influences?

9. Describe three ways in which persons and situations interact.

ANSWER KEY

Chapter Review

1. diversity
   similarities
   differences
   evolutionary
   cultural

2. natural
   genes
   universal

3. learn
   culture

4. rules
   grease
   personal
   more
   distance

5. universal
   status
   higher
   lower
   intimacy

6. norms
   superior
   subservient
   reversal

7. individualism
   independent
   collectivism
   interdependent

8. others
   personal

9. personal

   analytical
   holistically
   situation
   personality

10. expressions
    gestures
    facial
    emotions

11. understanding
    interpret

12. reality
    language

13. appreciation
    heritage
    culture

14. interdependent
    independent

15. expectations
    culture
    variations
    time
    peers

16. Biological
    cultural
    accentuate
    interact

17. interact
    react
    choose
    create

Matching Terms

1. m
2. l
3. j
4. n
5. d
6. f
7. a
8. i

9. o
10. g
11. b
12. h
13. c
14. e
15. k

True-False Review

1.	T	14.	F
2.	T	15.	F
3.	T	16.	F
4.	F	17.	T
5.	F	18.	F
6.	T	19.	T
7.	F	20.	F
8.	T	21.	F
9.	T	22.	T
10.	F	23.	F
11.	F	24.	T
12.	T	25.	T
13.	F		

Multiple-Choice Practice Test

1.	d	21.	d
2.	d	22.	d
3.	d	23.	a
4.	c	24.	b
5.	c	25.	b
6.	c	26.	c
7.	b	27.	c
8.	c	28.	a
9.	a	29.	d
10.	c	30.	d
11.	c	31.	b
12.	b	32.	a
13.	b	33.	b
14.	b	34.	b
15.	d	35.	c
16.	d	36.	a
17.	a	37.	a
18.	a	38.	d
19.	d	39.	c
20.	b	40.	d

CHAPTER 6
CONFORMITY

CHAPTER OBJECTIVES

After completing your study of this chapter you should be able to:

1. Define conformity
2. Explain the difference between compliance and acceptance.
3. Describe the findings of the Sherif, Asch, and Milgram classic studies on conformity.
4. Identify circumstances that are conducive to conformity.
5. Explain why people conform.
6. Describe how personality and cultural background contribute to conformity.
7. Explain why people sometimes resist social pressure.

CHAPTER REVIEW

Supply the words necessary to complete each of the following statements.

1. Conformity is a change in _____ or _____ as a result of real or imagined group _____.

2. Two of the many forms of conformity are _____, publicly acting in accord with social pressure while privately disagreeing and _____ which is both acting and believing in accord with social pressure.

CLASSIC STUDIES

3. Sherif found that estimates of the _____ phenomenon, the apparent movement of a stationary point of light in the dark, were easily influenced by the _____ of others. The group _____ lasted over long periods of time and succeeding generations of subjects.

4. Asch had individuals listen to others estimate which of three comparison _____ was equal to a standard. Although others gave an obviously _____ response, participants conformed 37 percent of the time.

5. Milgram investigated the degree to which people would obey an authority's instructions to deliver what were presumably traumatizing _____ _____ to another person in an adjacent room. Under optimum conditions — a _____, close-at-hand commander, a _____ victim, and no one else to exemplify disobedience — 65 percent of adult male participants fully complied.

6. The conformity studies illustrate at least three social-psychological principles discussed in earlier chapters: The impact of behaviour on _____, the power of the _____ to shape action, and the _____ attribution error.

WHEN DO PEOPLE CONFORM?

7. Conformity is influenced by several characteristics of the group. It is highest when the group is composed of _____ or more persons, is unanimous in its judgment, is cohesive, and the group is perceived as having high _____.

8. People also conform more when their responses are _____ and when they have not previously _____ themselves to a particular position.

WHY CONFORM?

9. People conform for two reasons: _____ influence is based on a person's desire to fulfill others' expectations, often to gain acceptance. _____ influence elicits conformity that results from accepting evidence about reality provided by other people.

WHO CONFORMS?

10. Researchers in the 1980s found that personality traits predict average social behaviours such as conformity when measured across many _____. Personality also predicts behaviour when the trait is _____ to a situation and when social influences are _____. _____ differences in conformity suggest that people can be socialized to be more or less socially responsive.

RESISTING SOCIAL PRESSURE

11. Blatant attempts at social coercion produce _____ — a motive to protect or restore one's sense of freedom. When group members simultaneously experience this motive, the result may be social _____.

12. People are uncomfortable when they appear too different from others, but neither do they want to appear the _____ as everyone else. Thus they will often act to preserve their sense of _____ and individuality.

MATCHING TERMS

Write the letter of the correct term from the right before the appropriate number on the left.

_____ 1. A "we feeling" — the extent to which members of a group are bound together, such as by attraction for one another.

_____ 2. Deciding to quit smoking after hearing that many more smokers develop lung cancer than do non-smokers.

_____ 3. A motive to protect or preserve one's sense of freedom.

_____ 4. Wearing jeans to school even though you find them uncomfortable.

_____ 5. The apparent movement of a stationary point of light in a dark room.

_____ 6. Studied obedience to authority.

_____ 7. A change in behaviour or belief influence as a result of real or imagined group pressure.

_____ 8. A soldier who shoots an enemy soldier because his captain told him to do it.

_____ 9. The underestimation of social forces.

_____ 10. An accomplice of the experimenter.

_____ 11. Used judgments of the lengths of lines to study conformity.

_____ 12. Conformity based on "going along to get along".

_____ 13. Used the autokinetic phenomenon to study how group norms encourage conformity.

a. conformity

b. Sherif

c. autokinetic phenomenon

d. confederate

e. Asch

f. compliance

g. Milgram

h. cohesiveness

i. normative influence

j. information influence

k. fundamental attribution error

l. reactance

m. obedience

TRUE-FALSE REVIEW

Circle T if the statement is true and F if it is false.

T F 1. Conformity is sometimes good and sometimes bad.

T F 2. Compliance and acceptance are different forms of conformity.

T F 3. A confederate who made an inflated estimate of the autokinetic phenomenon had no effect on the judgments of naive participants.

T F 4. Fatal auto accidents and private airplane crashes increase after well-publicized suicides.

T F 5. In Asch's study involving the judgment of length of lines, the correct answer was obvious.

T F 6. Asch's experimental procedure had "mundane" but not "experimental" realism.

T F 7. Milgram found that a total of 37 percent of male participants fully complied with the experimenter's commands.

T F 8. When surveyed afterwards, most of Milgram's participants said they regretted having volunteered to participate in his study.

T F 9. It is easier to abuse someone who is distant or depersonalized.

T F 10. When Milgram's experiment was repeated in a rundown office building in Bridgeport, the percentage of participants who fully complied to the commands of the experimenter remained unchanged.

T F 11. The conformity research indicates that evil has its basis in some character defect.

T F 12. Compliance can breed acceptance.

T F 13. Two groups of three people elicit more conformity than one group of six.

T F 14. Social impact theory has provided an explanation for why it is easier to debase someone who is distant or depersonalized.

T F 15. Group members who feel attracted to the group are more responsive to the group's influence.

T F 16. In the Milgram obedience studies, people of lower status tended to accept the experimenter's commands more readily than people of higher status.

T F 17. People conform more when they must respond in the presence of others than when allowed to write down their answers privately.

T F 18. In experiments on decision making by simulated juries, hung juries are more likely when jurors are polled by a show of hands rather than by secret ballot.

T F 19. Normative social influence results from a person's desire to find meaning in life.

T F 20. Informational influence encourages us to agree with what others say is right.

T F 21. Personality is more likely to predict average rather than specific behaviour.

T F 22. Knowing people's cultural backgrounds helps us predict how conforming they are.

T F 23. In more recent studies in Canada, university students still showed just as much conformity as in the original conformity studies.

T F 24. The theory of psychological reactance states that people desire consistency in their lives.

T F 25. When people are asked, "Tell us about yourself," they are most likely to report characteristics they share in common with others.

MULTIPLE-CHOICE PRACTICE TEST

Circle the correct letter.

1. _____ is a change in behaviour or belief as a result of group pressure.
   a. Cohesiveness
   b. Conformity
   c. Compliance
   d. Obedience

2. Publicly acting in accord with social pressure while privately disagreeing is called
   a. acceptance
   b. compliance
   c. reactance
   d. interaction

3. When people experience acceptance in response to social pressure they
   a. engage in actions consistent with the social pressure
   b. hold beliefs consistent with the social pressure
   c. they neither engage in actions nor hold beliefs consistent with the social pressure
   d. they both engage in actions and hold beliefs consistent with the social pressure

4. In using the autokinetic phenomenon, Jacobs and Campbell found that when a confederate gave an inflated estimate of movement
   a. naive participants were not influenced by the confederate's estimate
   b. naive participants who heard the estimate were influenced but new members who joined were not
   c. the confederate's judgment not only had an immediate influence but the effect persisted as original group members were replaced one at a time by new members
   d. the confederate's judgment had no immediate influence on group members but did have a delayed effect by shaping the estimates of group members after they left the group

5. Studies involving _____ most clearly demonstrate social influence taking the form of acceptance.
   a. judgments of the length of lines
   b. judgments of the autokinetic phenomenon
   c. shocking innocent victims
   d. administration of a drug overdose

6. Research has indicated that the number of suicides increases following
   a. well-publicized suicides
   b. a world war
   c. the Olympic games
   d. an economic recession

7. An important difference between Asch's experiment in which participants judged the length of lines and Sherif's experiment in which participants judged the movement of light was that
   a. Asch's participants were older than were Sherif's
   b. there was an obviously correct answer in judging the length of lines but that was not so in judging the movement of light
   c. Asch's participants made their judgments privately whereas Sherif's participants made their judgments publicly
   d. Asch's participants were all male whereas Sherif's participants were both male and female

8. In Asch's study of perceptual judgment involving the length of lines, naive participants conformed _____ of the time to the false judgments of the confederates.
   a. 10 percent
   b. 37 percent
   c. 68 percent
   d. 92 percent

9. A psychiatrist who interviewed 40 of Milgram's participants a year after their participation concluded that
   a. none had been harmed
   b. many were suspicious of all authorities
   c. a minority had lowered self-esteem
   d. most regretted having served in Milgram's study

10. Participants' tendencies to obey the experimenter's commands to shock a victim were highest when the experimenter was _____ and the victim was

   _____.
   a. close; distant
   b. close; close
   c. distant; distant
   d. distant; close

11. When hospital nurses were called by an unknown physician and ordered to administer an obvious overdose of a drug,
    a. the majority of nurses did not comply and reported the incident to their supervisor
    b. the inexperienced nurses complied while the more experienced challenged the order
    c. most indicated to the physician that he would have to come in to sign the order before they could comply
    d. all but one proceeded to comply without delay

12. George is about to enter the main college building when a man tells him, "You can't enter the building, there's a problem." George is most likely to obey if
    a. the man is very agitated
    b. the man is a campus security officer
    c. the man is a student
    d. the man is at least 35 years old

13. When the study of obedience was moved from Yale University to Bridgeport, Connecticut, the number of people who complied
    a. decreased from 65 percent to 48 percent
    b. decreased from 75 percent to 25 percent
    c. increased from 37 percent to 50 percent
    d. decreased from 37 percent to 10 percent

14. Milgram reported that a participant's tendency to obey the experimenter decreased dramatically
    a. when two other participants defied the experimenter
    b. when the participant could not hear the responses of the learner
    c. when the experimenter was a female
    d. when the experimenter was younger than the participant

15. How social pressure may lead us to perform immoral acts is best illustrated by studies of
    a. psychological reactance
    b. spontaneous self-concept
    c. obedience to authority
    d. informational influence

16. The training of torturers by the military junta in Greece in the early 1970s illustrates
    a. psychological reactance
    b. the inoculation effect
    c. the foot-in-the-door phenomenon
    d. the role of personality in conformity

17. In one experiment conducted by Swim and Hyers (1998) in which students were asked to predict how they would respond to a male's sexist comments, a _____ of students said they would ignore them. When other students actually heard such sexist remarks being made, a _____ of students said nothing.
    a. minority; minority
    b. minority; majority
    c. majority; minority
    d. majority; majority

18. Which of the following social-psychological principles is not illustrated by the conformity literature?
    a. behaviour shapes attitudes
    b. the fundamental attribution error
    c. the inoculation effect
    d. the power of the situation

19. To believe that Asch's compliant participants were particularly spineless people is to
    a. forget that behaviour shapes belief
    b. overlook other personality characteristics that determine conformity
    c. make the fundamental attribution error
    d. ignore how the status of the experimenter shapes behaviour

20. In light of the Milgram studies, to believe that soldiers who shoot innocent civilians as a consequence of following orders are unusually cruel is to
    a. make the fundamental attribution error
    b. engage in self-serving bias
    c. overlook the effect of cultural differences on conformity
    d. underestimate the influence of personality differences on conformity

21. Increasing the size of the group from _____ to _____ is likely to produce the greatest increase in conformity.
    a. 2 to 5
    b. 5 to 10
    c. 50 to 100
    d. 1000 to 2000

22. The effect of group size on conformity has been explained by _____ theory.
    a. cognitive dissonance
    b. social norm
    c. psychological reactance
    d. social impact

23. People who observed a lone individual in a group of four misjudge blue stimuli as green were subsequently
    a. more likely to conform to a group's erroneous judgments
    b. less likely to conform to a group's erroneous judgments
    c. less likely to value individualism
    d. more likely to value wisdom

24. Conformity is highest when the response is _____ and _____.
    a. private; made without prior commitment
    b. public; made without prior commitment
    c. nonverbal; made in response to inanimate objects
    d. insignificant; made with prior commitment

25. Politicians rarely shift their positions on major foreign policy matters. This may be an example of how
    a. a "we-they" feeling has emerged between the major political parties
    b. public commitment reduces susceptibility to social influence
    c. high self-esteem is strongly related to nonconformity
    d. emotional distance from victims leads to disregard for their welfare

26. Normative influence is to informational influence as _____ is to _____.
    a. autokinetic effect; cohesiveness
    b. compliance; acceptance
    c. conformity; reactance
    d. acceptance; reactance

27. _____ is based on a person's desire to be accepted by the group.
    a. Indirect influence
    b. Nominal influence
    c. Normative influence
    d. Informational influence

28. After hearing a respected medical authority lecture about the value of eating fresh fruits and vegetables, Joshua includes more of them in his diet. This change in Joshua's eating patterns is an example of
    a. normative social influence
    b. psychological reactance
    c. informational social influence
    d. social facilitation

29. Peter hates to wear ties anywhere. Nevertheless he wears one to his sister's wedding to avoid the disapproval of his family. This is an example of
    a. identification
    b. informational social influence
    c. normative social influence
    d. psychological reactance

30. _____ is based on a person's desire to be correct.
    a. Indirect influence
    b. Nominal influence
    c. Normative influence
    d. Informational influence

31. Which of the following is not true about cultural differences in conformity?
    a. strong evidence of conformity seems to exist in every culture
    b. there seem to be important differences in the level of conformity between cultures
    c. situational effects on conformity seem small compared to cultural differences
    d. people in collectivist countries show more conformity than people from individualistic countries

32. Research indicates that personality is a better predictor of behaviour when the people studied are _____ and when the social influences are _____.
    a. similar; strong
    b. similar; weak
    c. diverse; strong
    d. diverse; weak

33. When Asch's conformity experiment has been repeated in other countries, the highest rate of conformity has been found in
    a. Lebanon
    b. the Bantu of Zimbabwe
    c. Hong Kong
    d. Brazil

34. Compared to Euro-American cultures, Asian cultures are more likely to teach their children
    a. independence
    b. collectivism
    c. to follow their own conscience
    d. to respect another's privacy

35. Psychological reactance theory provides an explanation for
    a. resistance to authority
    b. obedience to authority
    c. why compliance is more common than acceptance
    d. why people are most likely to conform when the group is unanimous

36. Milly generally likes to go home to visit her family during vacation. However, after her father tells her she must be home during spring vacation, Milly decides to remain at college. We can probably best understand Milly's behaviour in terms of
    a. reaction formation
    b. regression
    c. psychological reactance
    d. self-serving bias

37. Studies of people's spontaneous self-concepts indicate that
    a. they see themselves as better than average
    b. they react to blatant social pressure
    c. females define themselves in terms of their similarities while males define themselves in terms of their differences
    d. people value their uniqueness

38. John has red hair, has two brothers, one sister, and was born in Chicago. Both his parents were born in this country and are lawyers. If you asked John to "tell us about yourself," he is most likely to mention that
    a. he has two brothers
    b. he has red hair
    c. his father has a college education
    d. he was born in this country

39. Ancient astronomers who observed the stars occasionally saw a star that seemed to move very abruptly. This is probably an example of
    a. the autokinetic effect
    b. the inoculation effect
    c. astronomical impact theory
    d. normative social influence

40. Philip hates to attend concerts but goes because his wife wants to. After three years Philip comes to genuinely enjoy concerts. This is an example of
    a. how acceptance can lead to compliance
    b. how compliance can lead to acceptance
    c. the "boomerang effect"
    d. how psychological reactance can lead to acceptance

SHORT ESSAY QUESTIONS

Answer the following questions in the space provided.

1. Define conformity. Explain the distinction between compliance and acceptance.

2. Briefly describe how each of the following investigators attempted to study conformity.

A. Sherif

B. Asch

C. Milgram

3. Identify three factors that are important to understanding <u>when</u> people conform.

4. Give two reasons <u>why</u> people conform.

5. Explain how personality and culture influences <u>who</u> conforms.

6. Give two explanations for why people sometimes resist influence.

ANSWER KEY

Chapter Review

1. behaviour
   belief
   pressure

2. compliance
   acceptance

3. autokinetic
   estimates
   norm

4. lines
   wrong

5. electric shocks
   legitimate
   remote

6. attitudes
   situation
   fundamental

7. three
   status

8. public
   committed

9. normative
   informational

10. situations
    specific
    weak
    Cultural

11. reactance
    rebellion

12. same
    uniqueness

Matching Terms

1. h
2. j
3. l
4. f
5. c
6. g
7. a
8. m
9. k
10. d
11. e
12. i
13. b

True-False Review

1. T
2. T
3. F
4. T
5. T
6. F
7. F
8. F
9. T
10. F
11. F
12. T
13. T
14. F
15. T
16. T
17. T
18. T
19. F
20. T
21. T
22. T
23. F
24. F
25. F

Multiple-Choice Practice Test

1.	b	21.	c
2.	b	22.	d
3.	d	23.	b
4.	c	24.	b
5.	b	25.	b
6.	a	26.	b
7.	b	27.	c
8.	b	28.	c
9.	a	29.	c
10.	a	30.	d
11.	d	31.	c
12.	b	32.	d
13.	a	33.	b
14.	a	34.	b
15.	c	35.	a
16.	c	36.	c
17.	b	37.	d
18.	c	38.	b
19.	c	39.	a
20.	a	40.	b

CHAPTER 7
PERSUASION

CHAPTER OBJECTIVES

After completing your study of this chapter you should be able to:

1. Identify the two routes to persuasion.
2. Describe communicator characteristics that contribute to effective communication.
3. Explain how the content of the message influences its effectiveness.
4. Describe the effects of different channels of communication.
5. Identify characteristics of the audience which influence susceptibility to persuasion.
6. Discuss the persuasion principles utilized in cult indoctrination.
7. Explain how people can resist persuasion.

CHAPTER REVIEW

Supply the words necessary to complete each of the following statements.

1. Powerful persuasive forces are at work in today's world influencing people's attitudes and behaviour. Because of health promotion campaigns in Canada, the smoking rate has _____ to about half the rate that it was 30 years ago.

2. However, not all persuasive efforts succeed. The attempt to persuade people to use _____ _____ has had not discernible effect.

TWO ROUTES TO PERSUASION

3. Central route persuasion occurs when interested people focus on _____ and respond with favorable _____. Peripheral route persuasion occurs when people use rule-of-thumb _____ or incidental _____ to make snap judgments.

THE ELEMENTS OF PERSUASION

4. The four factors extensively studied in research on persuasion have been the _____, the message, _____ the message is communicated, and the _____.

5. Credible communicators are both _____ and _____. People who speak _____ and look listeners straight in the eye are viewed as more credible. Trustworthiness is also increased if the audience believes the communicator is not trying to persuade them, argues against his or her own _____, and _____ fast.

6. _____ communicators, for example, those with physical appeal or who are similar to the audience, are also persuasive. Similar communicators are more effective on matters of _____ than on judgments of _____.

7. Messages are more convincing when associated with _____ _____. Messages that arouse _____ can also be effective especially when the listener is given effective ways to reduce it.

8. The effect of _____ depends on the communicator's credibility. Highly credible people elicit the most opinion change when they argue a relatively _____ position. Less credible people are more successful advocating a _____ position. Those highly _____ in an issue also tend to accept a narrow range of views.

9. A one-sided appeal is more effective than a two-sided appeal when the audience _____ with the message, and is _____ of opposing arguments.

10. In terms of arguments being presented first or last, the most common finding has been a _____ effect. However, when _____ separates the two messages and if a _____ must be made immediately after hearing the second side, a _____ effect is more likely.

11. Attitudes developed from active _____ are stronger than those shaped by appeals passively received. Although the mass media are typically not as potent as _____ influence, the media are effective when the issue is minor or _____. Many of the media's effects operate in a " _____ flow" of communication — from media to _____ leaders to the rank and file.

12. People with _____ self-esteem are the easiest to influence. The _____ of the audience is also important. We seem to form our basic attitudes when young and carry them through adulthood.

CASE STUDIES IN PERSUASION: CULT INDOCTRINATION

14. Cults strengthen members' commitment by utilizing the principle that compliance breeds
_____. By gradually increasing demands, the cult exploits the
_____ phenomenon.

15. Successful cults have a _____ leader and present a vivid,
_____ message that is directed to people who are at a _____
     point in their lives. The cult typically _____ members in like-minded
groups.

RESISTING PERSUASION: ATTITUDE INOCULATION

16. A prior public _____ to one's position, stimulated perhaps by a
_____ attack on the position, breeds resistance to later
persuasion. The attack on one's belief stimulates one to develop _____
that immunize against further attacks. This is known as attitude _____.

MATCHING TERMS

Write the letter of the correct term from the right before the appropriate number on the left.

_____ 1. Information presented first has the most influence.

_____ 2. Breeds counterarguing.

_____ 3. Produced by weak attacks on people's beliefs.

_____ 4. The impact of a noncredible person may increase over time.

_____ 5. Influential on matters of personal value.

_____ 6. Especially effective when coupled with specific recommendations.

_____ 7. Isolation from family and friends produces this.

_____ 8. Information presented last has the most influence

_____ 9. How the media influence the rank and file.

_____ 10. Face-to-face, in writing, on film.

_____ 11. Occurs when people are influenced by incidental cues.

_____ 12. Determines the effect of "discrepant" messages.

_____ 13. Marshals systematic arguments to stimulate favorable thinking.

a. sleeper effect

b. fear appeals

c. primacy effect

d. recency effect

e. communication channels

f. central route persuasion

g. attitude inoculation

h. communicator's credibility

i. social implosion

j. peripheral route persuasion

k. forewarning

l. two-step flow

m. similar communicators

TRUE-FALSE REVIEW

Circle T if the statement is true and F if it is false.

T F 1.   Collegians' support for marijuana's legalization continues to dwindle.

T F 2.   Several educational campaigns in different sections of the country have been successful in convincing motorists to use seat belts.

T F 3.   The central route to persuasion is best illustrated by advertisements that feature Hollywood stars.

T F 4.   The term "sleeper effect" refers to the fact that what people are doing when a message is presented influences its effectiveness.

T F 5.   Speakers who talk rapidly are generally seen as lacking in credibility.

T F 6.   Communicators are viewed as more trustworthy if the audience believes they are not trying to persuade them.

T F 7.   Dissimilar communicators are more effective than similar communicators on matters of objective reality.

T F 8.   Well-educated audiences are more responsive to rational appeals than are less-educated audiences.

T F 9.   Researchers found that college students were more convinced by persuasive messages if allowed to enjoy peanuts and Pepsi while reading them.

T F 10.   Messages are not effective if they evoke negative emotions.

T F 11.   A highly credible source elicits most opinion change by advocating a position moderately discrepant from the position held by the recipient.

T F 12.   Two-sided arguments are more effective than one-sided arguments if the listener initially disagrees with the communicator's position.

T F 13.   In terms of the order of arguments, a recency effect is more commonly found than a primacy effect.

T F 14. People rated trivial statements like "Mercury has a higher boiling point than copper" as more truthful if they had read and rated them a week before.

T F 15. Television advertisements for aspirin are generally ineffective.

T F 16. The "two-step flow of communication" model has been used to explain the mass media's effect on the audience.

T F 17. Messages are best comprehended and recalled when written.

T F 18. The life-cycle explanation offers the best account of the generation gap.

T F 19. Forewarning people that they will be exposed to a discrepant message reduces their susceptibility to it.

T F 20. Cult leaders use the foot-in-the-door technique to gain behaviour commitments.

T F 21. The group isolation that occurs in cults leads to "social implosion."

T F 22. Cult influence techniques are in some ways similar to techniques used by more familiar groups.

T F 23. Persuasion techniques used by cults have so much power almost all the people in the cult are caught under the leader's spell.

T F 24. "Attitude inoculation" is accomplished by offering people new arguments to bolster their existing attitudes.

T F 25. Being an active listener may build up one's resistance to persuasion.

MULTIPLE-CHOICE PRACTICE TEST

Circle the correct letter.

1. According to the text, persuasive attempts have probably been least effective in changing attitudes toward
    a. cigarette smoking
    b. marijuana use
    c. use of seat belts
    d. alcohol consumption

2. Social psychologists study persuasion primarily through
    a. experiments
    b. surveys
    c. case studies
    d. participant observation

3. The central route is to _____ as the peripheral route is to _____.
    a. analytical; motivated
    b. similarity; attractiveness
    c. heuristics; incidental cues
    d. high effort; low effort

4. Which of the following is one of the four major factors studied by psychologists in research on effective persuasion?
    a. the function of communication
    b. the setting of communication
    c. the channel of communication
    d. the length of communication

5. Credible communicators are perceived as both _____ and _____.
    a. expert; attractive
    b. intelligent; mature
    c. attractive; intelligent
    d. expert; trustworthy

6. Which of the following most clearly demonstrates the "sleeper effect"?
    a. unsuspecting people often fail to distinguish education from propaganda
    b. a foreign language can be acquired by listening to records while one sleeps
    c. the impact of a noncredible person may increase over time
    d. people who are not alert rarely counterargue

7. A gun manufacturer delivers a speech against stricter gun legislation. Because he clearly has a vested interest, his arguments have little initial impact on the audience. However, several weeks later, a survey of the audience indicates that his impact was much greater than first thought. This would be an example of
   a. the recency effect
   b. the sleeper effect
   c. social implosion
   d. attitude inoculation

8. Communicators who talk fast and look the listener in the eye are likely to be perceived as more
   a. selfish
   b. manipulative
   c. attractive
   d. credible

9. Wood and Eagly reported that when a speaker presents _____ we are more likely to attribute the message to compelling evidence and thus to be persuaded by it.
   a. a popular rather than an unpopular position
   b. an unexpected rather than an expected position
   c. an emotional rather than a rational appeal
   d. a political rather than a religious position

10. People who argue against their own self-interest
   a. are effective in persuading a female audience but not in persuading a male audience
   b. are effective with an intelligent audience but not with an unintelligent audience
   c. are viewed as inconsistent and thus lose their effectiveness
   d. are viewed as more credible and are thus more influential

11. "Similar" communicators are more effective in persuading on _____ than on _____.
   a. radio; television
   b. judgments of fact; matters of value
   c. political issues; religious beliefs
   d. matters of value; judgments of fact

12. An attractive or similar communicator would be most effective in changing beliefs about the
    a. health benefits of eating fruits and vegetables
    b. dangers of marijuana use
    c. dangers of driving without wearing seatbelts
    d. advantages of living in a small town versus the country or a large city

13. What is the effect of a fear-arousing communication?
    a. fear renders a communication ineffective
    b. generally the more frightened people are, the more they respond
    c. evoking a low level of fear is effective, but producing a high level of fear is not
    d. fear appeals are effective with women but boomerang with men

14. Dawn Wilson and her colleagues found that doctors' letters to patients who smoked were most influential if they explained that by
    a. continuing to smoke they would likely die sooner
    b. quitting they would live longer
    c. quitting their food would taste better
    d. quitting they would save money

15. You have been asked to design an advertising campaign urging people to stop drinking alcohol and you decide to use fear to persuade them. To be most effective your message should
    a. arouse a low level of fear
    b. arouse a moderate level of fear
    c. arouse a high level of fear
    d. provide people with a way to avoid the fear

16. Which factor has been shown to influence the impact a discrepant message has on the audience?
    a. age of the audience
    b. communication channel
    c. communicator credibility
    d. communicator attractiveness

17. Highly credible communicators elicit most opinion change when they advocate positions that
    a. differ only moderately from the position of the audience
    b. differ extensively from the position of the audience
    c. elicit strong reactance from the audience
    d. arouse strong dissonance in the audience

18. American World War II soldiers initially opposed to a message suggesting that the Japanese would not be easily defeated were more persuaded by a(n) _____ communication. Soldiers initially agreeing with the message were strengthened more by a _____ message.
    a. videotaped; written
    b. one-sided; two-sided
    c. emotional; rational
    d. two-sided; one-sided

19. You have been asked to prepare a speech opposing capital punishment. To be most effective in convincing those who strongly favor the death penalty you should present
    a. a one-sided communication
    b. a two-sided communication
    c. an emotional appeal
    d. an audio taped appeal

20. You are one of two candidates being interviewed for a position as superintendent of the city school system. You are notified that one candidate will be interviewed tomorrow evening and the other a week later. The school board will make a decision immediately after the second candidate has been interviewed. If you want the job
    a. you should try to be interviewed first
    b. you should try to be interviewed last
    c. you should try to be interviewed first but only if the school board is composed of college graduates and the other candidate is controversial
    d. you should try to be interviewed first but only if you are more attractive than the other candidate

21. When two persuasive messages are presented back-to-back and the audience responds at some later time,
    a. a primacy effect occurs
    b. a recency effect occurs
    c. a primacy effect occurs with rational appeals but a recency effect occurs with emotional appeals
    d. social implosion occurs

22. Persuasion studies have shown that the major influence upon our most important beliefs and attitudes is
    a. television and radio
    b. the school
    c. the church
    d. our contact with people

23. College students who live on campus report that they learn most from their contact with
    a. books
    b. professors
    c. newspapers and magazines
    d. friends and fellow students

24. Which of the following illustrates media influence through a two-step flow of communication?
    a. a teenager buys a shampoo he saw advertised both on television and in a favorite magazine
    b. a gun manufacturer convinces a television station to broadcast a program on the right of citizens to bear arms
    c. a candidate for political office answers questions from a live audience on television
    d. a salesman purchases a new car after talking to a respected friend who read about its advantages in a consumers' magazine

25. The mass media's persuasive power is most noticeable on
    a. religious beliefs
    b. matters of objective fact
    c. political values
    d. minor or unfamiliar issues

26. The results of one study indicated that easy-to-understand messages were most persuasive when _____ while difficult messages were most persuasive when _____.
    a. audiotaped; written
    b. written; presented live
    c. videotaped, written
    d. videotaped; audiotaped

27. According to research presented in the text, the mass media may be most effective in shaping
    a. whether one becomes a Democrat or Republican
    b. whether a person believes in God or not
    c. the brand of shampoo a person buys
    d. one's attitude toward capital punishment

28. Compared to people with high self-esteem, people with low self-esteem are
    a. easier to persuade
    b. harder to persuade
    c. neither easier nor harder to persuade
    d. more difficult to persuade, but only on attitudes related to the self

29. "Life-cycle" and "generational" explanations both attempt to explain
    a. why the content of messages changes over time
    b. why people have different attitudes depending on their age
    c. why a particular communicator has a different effect on people of different ages
    d. how an emotional appeal builds to a climax in terms of its impact

30. What effect does distraction have on persuasive communications?
    a. distraction interferes with reception of the message and as a result the communication is always less persuasive
    b. distraction facilitates persuasion by inhibiting counterarguing
    c. the results of studies are so conflicting that no one knows
    d. distraction facilitates persuasion by reducing the sleeper effect

31. People may be more likely to be influenced by peripheral cues such as the appeal of the communicator when they are
    a. image-conscious and thus care less about whether they are right or wrong
    b. highly involved in the issue
    c. analytically inclined
    d. in genuine conflict over the merits of the arguments

32. Forewarning people that they are going to be exposed to a persuasive communication
    a. distracts them and thus makes them more susceptible to influence
    b. generally has no effect on their susceptibility to influence
    c. elicits fear and reduces their comprehension of the message
    d. makes them more resistant to influence

33. People who are highly involved in an issue will likely be most strongly influenced by the
    a. attractiveness of the source
    b. expertise of the source
    c. strength of the arguments
    d. sheer number of arguments

34. Research indicates that stimulating thinking in the audience makes strong messages
    _____ persuasive and weak messages _____ persuasive.
    a. more; more
    b. more; less
    c. less; more
    d. less; less

35. According to cult researcher Margaret Singer, youths from which class may be most trusting
    and thus vulnerable to a "credible" communicator?
    a. lower class
    b. middle class
    c. upper class
    d. all are equally vulnerable

36. According to the text, which age group is most vulnerable to cult indoctrination?
    a. under age 25
    b. between 25 and 35
    c. between 35 and 45
    d. over 60

37. Social implosion occurs in groups when
    a. ties with people outside the group weaken and each member interacts only with other
       group members
    b. a cult member overthrows the leader
    c. the poorer members assume leadership and the wealthy become the followers
    d. the cult seeks to attempt major changes in society

38. Attitude inoculation seeks to strengthen beliefs
    a. by giving supporting arguments for the beliefs
    b. by using different channels to communicate the same message
    c. by providing social support for the beliefs
    d. through a weak attack on the beliefs

39. According to the text, the inoculation research suggests that one can build up resistance to
    persuasion by
    a. listening only to rational appeals
    b. seeking social support for one's beliefs
    c. being an active listener
    d. ignoring emotional appeals

40. Attitude inoculation probably helps people resist persuasive appeals because it
    a. causes people to become defensive in protecting their attitudes
    b. increases people's ability to counterargue against attitude discrepant arguments
    c. allows people to process information through the peripheral route to persuasion
    d. immunizes people against hearing the arguments made against their point of view

SHORT ESSAY QUESTIONS

Answer the following questions in the space provided.

1. Contrast the two routes to persuasion.

2. List the four major factors psychologists have investigated in research on persuasion.

3. What factors influence the perceived credibility of a communicator?

4. Briefly state the research findings regarding each of the following:

    A. Fear appeals

B. Message discrepancy

C. One-sided versus two-sided messages

D. Primacy versus recency effects

5. Contrast the effectiveness of face-to-face personal influence and that of the mass media.

6. Describe how the principles of effective persuasion are implemented in cult indoctrination.

7. Explain what is meant by attitude inoculation.

ANSWER KEY

Chapter Review

1. plunged
   abstain

2. seat belts

3. arguments
   thoughts
   heuristics
   cues

4. communicator
   how
   audience

5. expert
   trustworthy
   confidently
   self-interest
   talks

6. Attractive
   value
   fact

7. good feelings
   fear

8. discrepancy
   extreme
   moderate
   involved

9. agrees
   unaware

10. primacy
    time
    commitment
    recency

11. experience
    personal
    unfamiliar
    two-step
    opinion

12. moderate
    age

13. thinking
    Forewarning
    counterarguing
    distrating
    persuasion

14. acceptance
    foot-in-the-door

15. charismatic
    emotional
    turning
    isolates

16. commitment
    mild
    counterarguments
    innoculation

Matching Terms

1. c
2. k
3. g
4. a
5. m
6. b
7. i

8. d
9. l
10. e
11. j
12. h
13. f

True-False Review

1.	F	14.	T
2.	F	15.	F
3.	F	16.	T
4.	F	17.	T
5.	F	18.	F
6.	T	19.	T
7.	T	20.	T
8.	T	21.	T
9.	T	22.	T
10.	F	23.	F
11.	F	24.	F
12.	T	25.	T
13.	F		

Multiple-Choice Practice Test

1.	c	21.	a
2.	a	22.	d
3.	d	23.	d
4.	c	24.	d
5.	d	25.	d
6.	c	26.	c
7.	b	27.	c
8.	d	28.	c
9.	b	29.	b
10.	d	30.	b
11.	d	31.	a
12.	d	32.	d
13.	b	33.	c
14.	a	34.	b
15.	d	35.	b
16.	c	36.	a
17.	b	37.	a
18.	d	38.	d
19.	b	39.	c
20.	b	40.	b

CHAPTER 8
GROUP INFLUENCE

CHAPTER OBJECTIVES

After completing your study of this chapter you should be able to:

1. Define a group.
2. Discuss how we are affected by the presence of others.
3. Identify the conditions under which social loafing is likely to occur.
4. Describe the psychological state of "deindividuation."
5. Define and explain group polarization.
6. Discuss the causes, symptoms, and prevention of "groupthink."
7. Identify the factors that strengthen minority influence and describe effective leadership.

CHAPTER REVIEW

Supply the words necessary to complete each of the following statements.

WHAT IS A GROUP?

1. A group consists of _____ or more people who, for longer than a few moments, _____ with and influence one another and perceive one another as "us."

SOCIAL FACILITATION

2. The most elementary issue in social psychology concerns how we are affected by the mere _____ of other people. Some early experiments found that one's performance on simple arithmetic and verbal tasks _____ when either observers or coactors were present. Other experiments found that the presence of others can _____ one's performance.

3. Robert Zajonc reconciled the contradictory findings with a well-known principle from experimental psychology: arousal facilitates _____ responses. Subsequent research indicated that the presence of others boosts performance on _____ tasks and hinders performance on _____ tasks.

4. Being in a crowd intensifies people's normally _____ or _____ reactions. When sitting close together, we may be more responsive to people's reactions. Crowding also enhances _____.

5. Experiments suggest that we are aroused by others partly as a result of _____ apprehension and partly from a _____ between paying attention to others and paying attention to the task. Other studies indicate that the presence of others can be _____ even when the actor is not being evaluated or distracted.

SOCIAL LOAFING

6. Social loafing may occur in work situations where people pool their efforts toward a _____ goal and where individuals are not _____ for their efforts. Laboratory experiments show that group members work less hard when performing "_____ tasks." When responsibility is diffused, individuals may attempt to _____-ride on the group effort.

7. Research indicates that group members work hard when groups are given _____ objectives, when they are _____ for group success, and when there is a spirit of _____ to the team.

DEINDIVIDUATION

8. When high levels of social arousal are combined with diffused _____, people may abandon their normal restraints and lose their sense of _____ responsibility. Such "deindividuation" produces a feeling of _____ by being in a large group or by wearing uniforms.

9. The loss of self-awareness is accompanied by increased responsiveness to the immediate _____, be it positive or negative. Similarly, circumstances that increase _____ will decrease deindividuation.

GROUP POLARIZATION

10. James Stoner discovered that group decisions were usually _____. In seeking to explain the "risky shift," investigators discovered that discussion tends to _____ whatever is the initially dominant point of view.

11. Informational and normative influences explain why groups intensify _____. Group discussion elicits a pooling of persuasive _____ which favor the dominant point of view. In addition, social _____ with others reveals surprising support for one's initial inclination. To be perceived favorably, a person expresses stronger opinions.

GROUPTHINK

12. A group's desire for _____ can override its realistic appraisal of alternative courses of action. Irving Janis suggested that groupthink is most likely to occur when the group is cohesive, is _____ from contrary viewpoints, and has a _____ leader.

13. The symptoms of groupthink include (1) an _____ of invulnerability, (2) unquestioned belief in the group's _____, (3) rationalization, (4) _____ view of the opposition, (5) pressure to conform, (6) _____ of misgivings, (7) an illusion of unanimity, and (8) "_____" who protect the group from unpleasant information.

14. Groupthink can be prevented by encouraging critical _____ of all possible alternatives, by welcoming _____ from people outside the group and by openly discussing any lingering _____ concerning the group decision.

MINORITY INFLUENCE

15. Research indicates that a minority is most influential when it is _____ and persistent in its views, when its actions convey an image of _____, and when it elicits some defections from the majority. Even if it fails to persuade the majority to adopt its position, the minority may increase the majority's _____ and willingness to consider other alternatives.

16. One example of the power of individuals is _____, the process by which certain group members motivate and guide the group. Research indicates that effective supervisors score high on tests of both _____ and _____ leadership.

MATCHING TERMS

Write the letter of the correct term from the right before the appropriate number on the left.

_____ 1.   Occurs on additive tasks.

_____ 2.   Enhances a minority's influence.

_____ 3.   People who benefit from the group but give little in return.

_____ 4.   Occurs when groups suppress dissenting opinions and ideas.

_____ 5.   A way of evaluating one's opinions and abilities.

_____ 6.   The best supported explanation for group polarization.

_____ 7.   The process of mobilizing and guiding groups.

_____ 8.   Was revised in favor of group polarization.

_____ 9.   Occurs in groups that foster anonymity.

_____ 10. Tendency for group discussion to enhance individuals' initial leanings.

_____ 11. The strengthening of dominant responses due to the presence of others.

_____ 12. Partially explains why the presence of others arouses us.

_____ 13. A false impression of how others are thinking or feeling.

_____ 14. A symptom of groupthink.

a.   social comparison

b.   deindividuation

c.   free riders

d.   social facilitation

e.   social loafing

f.   evaluation apprehension

g.   risky shift

h.   self-censorship

i.   self-confidence

j.   informational influence

k.   group polarization

l.   pluralistic ignorance

m.   groupthink

n.   leadership

TRUE-FALSE REVIEW

Circle T if the statement is true and F if it is false.

T   F   1.   Social psychologists define a group as any collection of two or more individuals.

T   F   2.   "Coactors" are people engaged in some competitive activity.

T   F   3.   The social-facilitation effect has been explained in terms of informational influence.

T   F   4.   The presence of others facilitates the performance of easy tasks and hinders the performance of difficult tasks.

T   F   5.   College basketball players become slightly less accurate in their free-throw shooting in a packed field house.

T   F   6.   Whenever people are in a crowd, they experience discomfort and stress.

T   F   7.   Social loafing is not likely to occur in athletic contests where one individual competes against another.

T   F   8.   Social loafing seems to occur because of poor coordination of individual efforts within a group.

T   F   9.   Social loafing decreases when the size of a group increases.

T   F 10.   People in collectivist cultures exhibit more social loafing than do people in individualistic cultures.

T   F 11.   Anonymity inevitably has a negative impact on group members.

T   F 12.   Laboratory research suggests that putting on a black jersey can lead wearers to behave more aggressively.

T   F 13.   Deindividuation is synonymous with self-awareness.

T   F 14.   Research indicates that group discussion invariably increases risk taking.

T F 15. "Group polarization" refers to a split within a group.

T F 16. Group polarization may occur when members discover they share similar viewpoints.

T F 17. According to the text, the <u>Walkerton</u> disaster showed symptoms of groupthink.

T F 18. Recent research suggests that cohesiveness is a more significant determinant of groupthink than is directive leadership.

T F 19. One prescription for preventing groupthink is to have one or more members assigned the role of devil's advocate.

T F 20. The symptoms of groupthink illustrate the self-serving bias.

T F 21. Groups of eyewitnesses give accounts of a crime that are much more accurate than those provided by isolated individuals.

T F 22. Brainstorming in groups generates more creative ideas than do the same people working alone.

T F 23. Researchers have found that a minority person who defected from the majority was even more persuasive than one who consistently voiced the minority position.

T F 24. Researchers agree that all great leaders share common traits.

T F 25. Some research indicates that effective supervisors score high on tests of both task and social leadership.

MULTIPLE-CHOICE PRACTICE TEST

Circle the correct letter.

1. The definition of a group given in the text and provided by Marvin Shaw states that a group consists of
   a. any collection of individuals
   b. two or more people who interact and influence one another
   c. two or more people who share similar values
   d. a collection of individuals that is cohesive

2. Who of the following would be considered coactors?
   a. four people doing push-ups in an exercise class
   b. two people playing bridge
   c. eight competitors running a 5-kilometer race
   d. two children playing badminton

3. Which of the following is least likely to be considered a group as defined in the text?
   a. a husband and wife talking over dinner
   b. a committee of eight discussing the problem of neighborhood crime
   c. four seven-year-olds playing hide-and-go-seek
   d. seven people waiting at a bus stop

4. Which form of social influence discussed in Chapter 8 does not necessarily involve an interacting group?
   a. group polarization
   b. groupthink
   c. minority influence
   d. social facilitation

5. Early experiments found that the presence of others improved people's efficiency at
   a. learning nonsense syllables
   b. crossing out designated letters
   c. performing complex multiplication problems
   d. learning foreign language words

6. The presence of others would be most likely to improve performance on
   a. raking up leaves
   b. solving crossword puzzles
   c. learning foreign language words
   d. solving complex mathematical puzzles

7. James Michaels and his colleagues found that in the presence of observers,
    a. good pool players shot better and poor pool players shot worse
    b. students playing checkers and chess played worse
    c. good pool players shot worse and poor pool players shot better
    d. students playing checkers played better and students playing chess played worse

8. Studies of the effect of other people on athletic performance have shown that
    a. college basketball players become slightly more accurate when highly aroused by a packed field house
    b. the drives of professional golfers are shorter when an audience is present
    c. home teams in baseball's World Series have won 60 percent of the final games
    d. in college and professional sports, home teams win about 6 in 10 games

9. The presence of others would be least likely to improve performance in
    a. playing chess
    b. weightlifting
    c. running
    d. the broad jump

10. Research indicates that being in a crowd _____ positive reactions and _____ negative reactions.
    a. intensifies; intensifies
    b. weakens; intensifies
    c. intensifies; weakens
    d. weakens; weakens

11. In a study of university students in India, researchers found that crowding hampered performance only on _____ tasks.
    a. verbal
    b. motor
    c. simple
    d. complex

12. Research indicates that people perform best when their coactor is
    a. not watching them
    b. slightly superior
    c. of the opposite sex
    d. highly competitive

13. Which of the following is true?
    a. people's color preferences are stronger when they make judgments with others present
    b. ants excavate less sand in the presence of other ants
    c. in the presence of others, students take more time to learn a simple maze and less time to learn one that is complex
    d. joggers run more slowly when jogging with someone else

14. Social loafing would be least likely to occur
    a. in a boys' club trying to raise money by holding a Saturday car wash
    b. in a relay race where each team member's performance is timed
    c. in a community garden where each family is expected to contribute whatever free time they have
    d. in a work crew building a new highway

15. Social facilitation and social loafing have been explained in terms of difference in
    a. evaluation concern
    b. informational influence
    c. cognitive dissonance
    d. group polarization

16. Experiments show that people in groups loaf less when
    a. the task is challenging
    b. they are in an unfamiliar setting
    c. they have a strong sense of external control
    d. the task is routine

17. Which of the following is false?
    a. groups of friends loaf less than groups of strangers
    b. Israel's communal kibbutz farms have outproduced Israel's noncollective farms
    c. research completed in Japan, Thailand, and India indicates that social loafing does not occur in less individualistic, more group-centered cultures
    d. students pumped exercise bikes more energetically when they knew they were being individually monitored than when they thought their output was being pooled with that of other riders

18. Which process helps explain both social loafing and deindividuation?
    a. self-censorship
    b. minority influence
    c. diffusion of responsibility
    d. group polarization

19. After an exciting soccer game in which the home team loses, a crowd of fans throws garbage and begins to tear up the field. This behaviour is best understood in terms of
    a. group polarization
    b. deindividuation
    c. groupthink
    d. social facilitation

20. Women dressed in Ku Klux Klan-style coats and hoods were more aggressive than those who were visible and wearing name tags. This finding is best explained in terms of the process of
    a. groupthink
    b. deindividuation
    c. reactance
    d. social facilitation

21. Frank and Gilovich's laboratory research suggested that putting on a black uniform can produce
    a. social loafing
    b. groupthink
    c. aggression
    d. evaluation apprehension

22. The research on deindividuation shows that a group experience that diminishes people's self-consciousness also tends to
    a. decrease their emotional arousal
    b. disconnect their behaviour from their attitudes
    c. increase their feelings of self-esteem
    d. increase their sensitivity to social expectations

23. The term "risky shift" was used to refer to the finding of
    a. groups being riskier than individuals
    b. individuals being riskier than groups
    c. males being riskier than females
    d. people becoming less risky as they grow older

24. Studies of the risky shift eventually led to the formulation of
    a. social comparison theory
    b. the group polarization phenomenon
    c. the social facilitation effect
    d. the social loafing effect

25. Individuals who tend to favor stiff penalties for drunk drivers come together to discuss various ways of dealing with the problem of intoxicated drivers. The group polarization phenomenon predicts that after group discussion,
    a. the individuals will favor even more severe penalties for drunk drivers
    b. the individuals will tend to become more tolerant of drunk drivers
    c. the individuals will be divided into two opposing groups as to the best way to deal with drunk drivers
    d. the individuals will favor a rehabilitation program rather than a jail sentence for drunk drivers

26. Myers and Bishop set up groups of relatively prejudiced and unprejudiced high school students and asked them to respond both before and after discussion to issues involving racial attitudes. Results indicated that after discussion
    a. both groups were more prejudiced
    b. both groups were less prejudiced
    c. the individuals who were relatively unprejudiced became even less prejudiced and the individuals who were relatively prejudiced became even more prejudiced
    d. the individuals who were relatively unprejudiced became more prejudiced and the individuals who were relatively prejudiced became less prejudiced

27. Group polarization is most likely to occur in a group
    a. of like-minded people
    b. of unintelligent people
    c. of persons with differing value systems
    d. discussing political issues

28. An analysis of terrorist organizations around the world suggests that the extremist activities of these groups may be understood in terms of the process of
    a. social loafing
    b. social facilitation
    c. minority influence
    d. group polarization

29. According to the text, the best explanation for group polarization is
    a. social comparison theory
    b. informational influence
    c. diffusion of responsibility
    d. cognitive dissonance theory

30. Groupthink occurs when group members desire
    a. control
    b. harmony
    c. power
    d. freedom

31. Which of the following is not a symptom of groupthink?
    a. unquestioned belief in the group's morality
    b. rationalization
    c. conformity pressure
    d. social loafing

32. Which of the following is a comment you are least likely to hear made within a group characterized by groupthink?
    a. "Our critics are not very smart."
    b. "Our past decisions have always been right."
    c. "Let's make the decision and get out of here. I've got more important things to do."
    d. "It seems to me we are all in agreement on this, so let's proceed."

33. Which of the following is not an example of a symptom of groupthink displayed in the Walkerton water crisis?
    a. reporting the results of the tainted water to the Ministry of Environment
    b. the water treatment employees' belief that the water was safe
    c. even though they knew the water tested positive for contaminants, the water treatment employees believed that it wasn't the water that was making people sick
    d. when it was decided not to chlorinate the water, Frank Koebel did not object even though he knew this could lead to problems

34. A directive leader is a contributing cause of
    a. deindividuation
    b. responsibility diffusion
    c. groupthink
    d. the risky shift

35. Patrick Laughlin reported that if only two members of a six-person group are initially correct in solving an analogy problem, they
    a. rarely convince the others
    b. convince the others one-third of the time
    c. convince the others two-thirds of the time
    d. always convince the others

36. Moscovici and his associates found that if a minority judges blue slides to be green,
    a. it has no effect on the judgments of the majority
    b. members of the majority will occasionally agree but only if the minority is consistent
    c. members of the majority demonstrate reactance by judging green slides to be blue
    d. female but not male members of the majority will occasionally agree

37. Research suggests that minorities are less persuasive regarding _____ than regarding
    _____.
    a. fact; attitude
    b. attitude; fact
    c. principle; practice
    d. practice; principle

38. Research indicates that a minority member who _____ is persuasive.
    a. wavers
    b. has defected from the majority
    c. tends to be introverted
    d. appears impatient

39. Tom, a successful foreman in a large furniture factory, emphasizes the attainment of
    production goals and sets high standards for the workers under him. Tom's style is an
    example of _____ leadership.
    a. normative
    b. task
    c. autocratic
    d. social

40. Studies done in India, Taiwan, and Iran found that the most effective supervisors in coal
    mines, banks, and government offices scored
    a. high on both task and social leadership
    b. high on task and low on social leadership
    c. high on either task or social leadership but not high on both
    d. low on task and high on social leadership

SHORT ESSAY QUESTIONS

Answer the following questions in the space provided.

1. Distinguish between a collection of individuals and a group.

2. Describe how the meaning of the term "social facilitation" has changed.

3. Explain what is meant by "social loafing" and "free riders." When is free riding most likely to occur?

4. What is deindividuation? Briefly describe its causes and effects.

5. Provide two explanations for group polarization.

6. List the major symptoms of groupthink.

7. Identify two factors that contribute to the effectiveness of minority influence.

ANSWER KEY

Chapter Review

1. two
   interact

2. presence
   improved
   hinder

3. dominant
   easy
   complex

4. positive
   negative
   arousal

5. evaluation
   conflict
   arousing

6. common
   accountable
   additive
   free

7. challenging
   rewarded
   commitment

8. responsibility
   individual
   anonymity

9. situation
   self-awareness

10. riskier
    enhance

11. opinions
    arguments
    comparison

12. harmony
    isolated
    directive

13. illusion
    morality
    stereotyped
    self-censorship
    mindguards

14. evaluation p.280
    critiques
    doubts

15. consistent
    self-confidence
    self-doubts

16. leadership
    task
    social

Matching Terms

1. e
2. i
3. c
4. m
5. a
6. j
7. n

8. g
9. b
10. k
11. d
12. f
13. l
14. h

True-False Review

1. F
2. F
3. F
4. T
5. T
6. F
7. T
8. F

9. F
10. F
11. F
12. T
13. F
14. F
15. F
16. T

17.	T		22.	F
18.	F		23.	T
19.	T		24.	F
20.	T		25.	T
21.	T			

Multiple-Choice Practice Test

1.	b		21.	c
2.	a		22.	b
3.	d		23.	a
4.	d		24.	b
5.	b		25.	a
6.	a		26.	c
7.	a		27.	a
8.	d		28.	d
9.	a		29.	b
10.	a		30.	b
11.	d		31.	d
12.	b		32.	c
13.	a		33.	a
14.	b		34.	c
15.	a		35.	c
16.	a		36.	b
17.	c		37.	a
18.	c		38.	b
19.	b		39.	b
20.	b		40.	a

CHAPTER 9
ALTRUISM: HELPING OTHERS

CHAPTER OBJECTIVES

After completing your study of this chapter you should be able to:
1. Define altruism.
2. Describe how social-exchange theory explains altruism.
3. Analyze the social norms of reciprocity and social-responsibility that may motivate altruism.
4. Explain how evolutionary psychology accounts for altruism.
5. Discuss situational influences which enhance helpfulness.
6. Discuss personal influences that affect helping.
7. Identify who is likely to receive help.
8. Discuss how altruism can be increased.

CHAPTER REVIEW

Supply the words necessary to complete each of the following statements.
1. Altruism is a motive to increase another's _____ without conscious regard for one's _____ - _____ .

WHY DO WE HELP?

2. Social-exchange theory states that helping, like other social behaviors, is guided by social _____ in which we aim to maximize our _____ and minimize our _____ . Rewards for helping may be either _____ (for example, social approval) or _____ (for example, reducing one's own distress). Other psychologists believe that seeing another's suffering may lead us to feel _____ as well as distress and then our helping may be motivated by genuine _____ .

3. Researchers have identified two social norms that seem to motivate altruism. The _____ norm is an expectation that people will help, not hurt, those who have helped them. The norm applies most strongly to our interactions with our equals. The social-_____ norm is an expectation that people will help those dependent upon them. We apply this norm selectively by giving aid only to those who we believe _____ it.

4. Evolutionary psychology contends that the essence of life is gene _____ and thus we are programmed to be selfish. However, two forms of altruism that are favored by natural selection are _____ protection and _____ . Most evolutionary psychologists believe that, since people are born selfish, we must _____ altruism.

5. The three theories of altruism _____ one another in offering different levels of explanation. Yet each is vulnerable to charges of being speculative and of merely explaining-by-_____.

WHEN WILL WE HELP?

6. As the number of bystanders at an emergency increases, any given bystander is less likely to _____ the incident, less likely to _____ it as an emergency, and less likely to assume _____ for intervening. This is especially true when the situation is _____ and the other bystanders are _____ who cannot easily detect one another's alarm.

7. People are more likely to help after seeing someone else _____ and when they are not in a _____.

8. People are _____ willing to help after transgressing, apparently in order to relieve private _____ and to restore a positive public image. People who are in a _____ mood also tend to be altruistic when being helpful is a way of altering their mood. This "feel bad–do good" effect is generally not found in _____. Finally, people who are in a _____ mood are consistently more helpful.

9. Early research found only _____ relationships between personality variables and helping. The _____ of person and situation is clearly seen in research that compares the helpfulness of males and females.

WHOM DO WE HELP?

10. We are most likely to help those who both need and _____ it and those who are _____ to us. In crisis situations, women receive _____ offers of help than men, especially from men.

HOW CAN WE INCREASE HELPING?

11. One way to promote altruism is to _____ those factors that inhibit altruism. According to the decision tree, assisting people to _____ an incident correctly, and to assume _____ for intervening, should increase their involvement. Research shows that _____ asking people for help and making them more _____-aware promotes altruism.

12. Reprimands and the door-in-the-_____ technique promote helping by evoking _____ feelings and concern for one's self-image.

13. We can also _____ altruism. For example, research indicates that television's prosocial _____ have even greater effects on children than its antisocial models.

14. The _____ effect suggests that we should not use excessive rewards or threats in socializing altruism. If people are provided with just enough justification to help, they will view themselves as _____ persons and be more helpful. Finally, students who _____ about altruism are more helpful.

MATCHING TERMS

Write the letter of the correct term from the right before the appropriate number on the left.

_____ 1. An expectation that people will help those dependent upon them.

_____ 2. The classic illustration of altruism.

_____ 3. A person is less likely to provide help when others are present.

_____ 4. Seeing another's suffering may produce this.

_____ 5. Altruism that promotes gene survival.

_____ 6. Concern for one's self-image makes this effective.

_____ 7. Noticing, interpreting, assuming responsibility.

_____ 8. May prevent people who have helped from feeling altruistic.

_____ 9. The motivation to increase one's own welfare.

_____ 10. An effective means of socializing altruism.

_____ 11. Overestimating others' ability to read our emotions.

_____ 12. An expectation that people will help, not hurt, those who have helped them.

_____ 13. Perceiving certain individuals as outside the boundary within which one applies rules of fairness.

a. door-in-the-face technique

b. overjustification effect

c. bystander effect

d. egoism

e. kin selection

f. moral exclusion

g. social-responsibility norm

h. reciprocity norm

i. decision tree

j. modeling

k. the Good Samaritan

l. empathy

m. illusion of transparency

TRUE-FALSE REVIEW

Circle T if the statement is true and F if it is false.

T F 1. People will donate more money to a charity when offered a product such as candy or candles.

T F 2. Psychologists are in agreement that all our behavior is ultimately aimed at our own welfare.

T F 3. Social exchange theory predicts that we will often help others even if we do not get any reward for helping.

T F 4. The reciprocity norm encourages people to help anyone in need.

T F 5. The social-responsibility norm is an expectation that people will help those who have helped them.

T F 6. Evolutionary psychology favours altruism towards one's children rather than altruism towards one's parents.

T F 7. Compared to fraternal twins, genetically identical twins are noticeably more mutually supportive.

T F 8. Compared to people in nonurban areas, those in big cities are less willing to do small favours.

T F 9. In contrast to the other theories of altruism, the social norms theory is speculative and after-the-fact.

T F 10. As the number of bystanders increases, any given bystander is less likely to interpret an incident as an emergency.

T F 11. Choosing the form that assistance should take is one of the important steps in Latané and Darley's decision tree.

T F 12. According to the text, the "feel bad–do good" phenomenon does not apply to the elderly.

T F 13. Self-focused grief promotes altruism.

T F 14. Happiness makes people self-focused and thus less willing to help.

T F 15. When faced with potentially dangerous situations in which strangers need help, men are more likely to help than are women.

T F 16. Female helpers are more likely to assist female victims than male victims.

T F 17. Men more frequently help attractive women than those they see as unattractive.

T F 18. People consistently help those of the same race more readily than those of a different race.

T F 19. When we feel guilty we are more likely to help those around us.

T F 20. Altruism increases when one expects later to meet and to talk with a victim and other witnesses.

T F 21. Research indicated that participants who had just completed a biographical questionnaire were more willing to help.

T F 22. The door-in-the-face technique is a strategy for increasing altruism.

T F 23. Moral inclusion encourages altruistic behaviour.

T F 24. Research indicates that television's prosocial models actually have greater effects on viewers than its antisocial models have.

T F 25. One of the most effective ways of teaching altruism is through utilizing the overjustification effect.

MULTIPLE-CHOICE PRACTICE TEST

Circle the correct letter.

1. According to the text, the classic illustration of altruism is provided by
   a. the Kitty Genovese case
   b. the parable of the Good Samaritan
   c. the parable of the Prodigal Son
   d. President Lincoln's Emancipation Proclamation

2. "Social economics" is a term most closely associated with
   a. social norms theory
   b. evolutionary psychology
   c. social-exchange theory
   d. the decision tree

3. According to social-exchange theory we will help when
   a. the benefits are external and the costs are internal
   b. the benefits are greater than the costs
   c. the benefits and costs are proportional
   d. the benefits are smaller than the costs

4. According to Daniel Batson, genuine altruism may have its basis in feelings of
   a. happiness
   b. sadness
   c. guilt
   d. empathy

5. Researchers who have investigated the relationship between empathy and altruism
   a. agree that empathy leads to genuine altruism
   b. agree that empathy leads to helping that is egoistically motivated
   c. agree that empathy leads to pure altruism in females but not in males
   d. debate whether empathy leads to pure altruism

6. According to sociologist Alvin Gouldner, a universal moral code is
   a. a norm of reciprocity
   b. a norm of social responsibility
   c. kin selection
   d. a norm of restitution

7. The reciprocity norm applies
   a. most strongly to interactions with our superiors
   b. when affirmative action favours one group over another
   c. when people are able to repay a favour
   d. when one partner gives and the other takes

8. The social-responsibility norm is an expectation that people will
   a. help those dependent on them
   b. help those who have helped them
   c. assume responsibility for helping their parents
   d. assume responsibility for correcting past mistakes

9. The statement, "There is no duty more indispensable than that of returning a kindness," reflects the _____ norm.
   a. restitution
   b. reciprocity
   c. social-responsibility
   d. equity

10. Rewards and costs are to _____ as gene survival is to _____.
    a. social-exchange theory; social norms theory
    b. sociobiology; social norms theory
    c. social norms theory; evolutionary psychology
    d. social-exchange theory; evolutionary psychology

11. From an evolutionary perspective it would be most difficult to explain why
    a. John paid his son's hospital bill
    b. Phyllis helps her mother clean the house
    c. William helps his next-door neighbor paint his house
    d. Ruth risked her life to save a stranger from being murdered

12. According to the text, one possible reason why people in big cities are less helpful is that
    a. they have not internalized the norm of social responsibility
    b. they are busier than those living in small towns
    c. they have a greater number of selfish genes
    d. reciprocity does not work as well in big cities as it does in small, isolated groups

13. Since we are born selfish, evolutionary psychologists propose that we attempt to
    a. develop a drug that will encourage altruism
    b. develop an "altruistic gene"
    c. teach altruism
    d. live only in small, isolated communities

14. According to the text, which theory of altruism proposes two types of altruism: a tit-for-tat reciprocal exchange, and a more unconditional helpfulness?
    a. social norms theory
    b. evolutionary psychology
    c. social-exchange theory
    d. all of the above

15. Latané and Darley attempted to explain people's failure to intervene in cases like that of Kitty Genovese in terms of
    a. a situational influence
    b. a personality trait
    c. a mood factor
    d. selfish genes

16. Researchers had participants fill out a questionnaire in a room either by themselves or with two strangers. When the experimenters pumped smoke through a wall vent, solitary participants
    a. noticed the smoke more quickly than did those in groups
    b. were more likely to misinterpret the smoke as being truth gas
    c. were less likely to seek help
    d. finished the questionnaire more quickly

17. Which of the following is not one of the steps in Darley and Latané's decision tree?
    a. noticing the incident
    b. interpreting the incident as an emergency
    c. weighing the costs and benefits of helping
    d. assuming responsibility for intervening

18. You trip over a fallen branch and sprain your ankle. According to research on the bystander effect, a stranger who sees your plight will be most likely to offer aid if there are _____ others present.
    a. no
    b. two
    c. four
    d. ten

19. When his car overheated on a nearly deserted highway early one morning, elderly Mr. Hurley received help from the first passerby. One week later the same thing happened in the afternoon when traffic was heavy and Mr. Hurley waited nearly two hours for help. This difference best illustrates
    a. the overjustification effect
    b. social facilitation
    c. the illusion of transparency
    d. the bystander effect

20. The misinterpretations of emotional states involved in the bystander effect are fed by
    a. an illusion of transparency
    b. an illusion of control
    c. illusory correlation
    d. the foot-in-the-door phenomenon

21. Latané and Darley propose that one reason why bystanders make it harder to interpret an event as an emergency is that they
    a. cause diffusion of responsibility
    b. lead people to emphasize the costs of helping
    c. provoke pluralistic ignorance about the nature of the event
    d. discourage people from fulfilling their norm of social responsibility

22. What is meant by the term "bystander effect"?
    a. people are likely to gather at the scene of a serious accident
    b. people are likely to gather at the scene of a fire and hinder rescue operations
    c. people are more likely to provide aid when there are helping models present
    d. people are less likely to provide help when there are other bystanders

23. According to the text, the presence of others may not inhibit helping if the bystanders
    a. can read each other's reactions
    b. are all of the same sex
    c. have a high level of education
    d. are members of one of the helping professions

24. When participants in Darley and Latané's seizure experiment were later interviewed,
    a. most said they thought the deception used by the experimenter was justified but they would not be willing to take part in future similar experiments because of the stress
    b. most said they did not think the deception was justified but they would take part in future similar experiments
    c. most said they did not think the deception was justified and they would not take part in future similar experiments
    d. all said they thought the deception was justified and would be willing to take part in future similar experiments

25. According to the text, people in a hurry may be less willing to help because
    a. they have weighed the costs of helping and have decided they are too high
    b. they never fully grasp the situation as one requiring their assistance
    c. they tend to be selfish and primarily concerned with meeting their own needs
    d. they tend to be in a negative mood state and therefore are less likely to help

26. Which of the following negative moods is most likely to motivate altruism?
    a. depression
    b. anger
    c. guilt
    d. grief

27. Research indicates that compared to adults, young children are
    a. more likely to help
    b. less likely to help when they are busy
    c. less likely to help when they are sad
    d. less likely to help when they are watching television

28. Who of the following is least likely to help an injured pedestrian?
    a. Peter who has just found $10 in a grocery store
    b. Anita who is five minutes late for a committee meeting
    c. Carol who has just lost a dollar bill in a poker game
    d. Ralph who is five minutes early for work

29. Research suggests that we are especially likely to help when
    a. we are happy
    b. others are present and are doing nothing
    c. the potential recipient of our help is of the opposite sex
    d. the potential recipient of our help is of a different nationality

30. In comparison to low self-monitors, high self-monitors are especially helpful if
    a. they are led to think that helpfulness will be socially rewarded
    b. the social-responsibility norm is salient
    c. they are exposed to altruistic models
    d. they experience empathy

31. Research suggests that those who are high in _____ are more likely to be helpful.
    a. authoritarianism
    b. self-efficacy
    c. extroversion
    d. achievement motivation

32. What does research indicate regarding the role of gender difference in predicting helping?
    a. gender is unrelated to helping
    b. males are more helpful than females
    c. females are more helpful than males
    d. gender difference interacts with the situation

33. According to the text, the door-in-the-face technique works to promote altruism because people are
    a. provided a helpful model to imitate
    b. in a happy mood
    c. concerned about their self-image
    d. distracted from self-concern

34. When a solicitor for a charitable cause added the phrase, "Even a penny will help" to the request for a donation,
    a. the total number of contributors increased but the average amount of each contribution decreased
    b. both the number of contributors and the average amount of each contribution decreased
    c. both the number of contributors and the average amount of each contribution increased
    d. the total number of contributors decreased but the average amount of each contribution increased

35. Your roommate asks you to loan her twenty-five dollars to buy her boyfriend a birthday present and you refuse. She then asks for three dollars to purchase a new notebook. You loan her the three dollars. Your roommate has successfully used the
    a. overjustification effect
    b. insufficient justification effect
    c. door-in-the-face technique
    d. foot-in-the-door technique

36. Which of the following religious teachings most clearly promotes "moral inclusion"?
    a. "Love your neighbor as yourself"
    b. "Everyone is a child of God and thus your brother or sister"
    c. "Honor your father and your mother"
    d. "An eye for an eye and a tooth for a tooth"

37. In socializing altruism, we should beware of the
    a. overjustification effect
    b. underjustification effect
    c. fundamental attribution error
    d. foot-in-the-door effect

38. Which of the following techniques should elementary schoolteachers use if they hope to promote enduring altruistic tendencies in students?
    a. show them films of heroes who risked their own welfare to help others
    b. offer a prize to the boy or girl who is most helpful to other students in a two-week period
    c. reprimand and punish any overt aggression
    d. instill a sense of patriotism

39. Batson found that those who attributed their helpful act to compliance rather than compassion
    a. subsequently volunteered less time to a service agency
    b. demonstrated reactance and ended up feeling more empathy for the person they helped
    c. felt guilty and responded more positively to a new request for help
    d. were subsequently more aware of the reciprocity norm

40. Research has indicated that when students have been informed through a lecture of how bystanders can affect one's reactions to an emergency, the
    a. students are subsequently more likely to help someone in need
    b. students' willingness to help is unchanged for they refuse to believe they can be influenced by other people
    c. students' willingness to help is increased for a few hours following the lecture but for no longer
    d. students' willingness to help actually decreases due to psychological reactance

SHORT ESSAY QUESTIONS

Answer the following questions in the space provided.

1. Define altruism.

2. Explain how egoism and empathy can motivate helping according to the social exchange theory?

3. Identify two social norms that may motivate altruism and briefly explain each.

4. What two kinds of altruism are predicted by evolutionary psychology? Give a specific example of each.

5. Describe the steps in the decision tree for helping.

6. What is the relationship between mood and willingness to help?

7. What is the relationship between personality and willingness to help?

8. Describe whom we are most likely to help.

9. How can altruism be socialized?

ANSWER KEY

Chapter Review

1. welfare
   self-interests

2. economics
   rewards
   costs
   external
   internal
   empathy
   altruism

3. reciprocity
   responsibility
   deserve

4. survival
   kin
   reciprocity
   teach

5. complement
   naming

6. notice
   interpret
   responsibility
   ambiguous
   strangers

7. helping
   hurry

8. more
   guilt
   negative
   children
   positive

9. modest
   interaction

10. deserve
    similar
    more

11. reverse
    interpret
    responsibility
    personally
    self

12. face
    guilt

13. teach
    models

14. overjustification
    caring p.324
    learn p.324

Matching Terms

1. g
2. k
3. c
4. l
5. e
6. a
7. i

8. b
9. d
10. j
11. m
12. h
13. f

True-False Review

1.	T	14.	F
2.	F	15.	T
3.	F	16.	F
4.	F	17.	T
5.	F	18.	F
6.	T	19.	T
7.	T	20.	T
8.	T	21.	T
9.	F	22.	T
10.	T	23.	T
11.	F	24.	T
12.	F	25.	F
13.	F		

Multiple-Choice Practice Test

1.	b	21.	c
2.	c	22.	d
3.	b	23.	a
4.	d	24.	d
5.	d	25.	b
6.	a	26.	c
7.	c	27.	c
8.	a	28.	b
9.	b	29.	a
10.	d	30.	a
11.	d	31.	b
12.	d	32.	d
13.	c	33.	c
14.	d	34.	c
15.	a	35.	c
16.	a	36.	b
17.	c	37.	a
18.	a	38.	a
19.	d	39.	a
20.	a	40.	a

CHAPTER 10
AGGRESSION: HURTING OTHERS

CHAPTER OBJECTIVES

After completing your study of this chapter you should be able to:

1. Define aggression.
2. Differentiate between hostile and instrumental aggression.
3. Discuss the instinct view of aggression.
4. Describe biological influences on aggression.
5. Identify the causes and consequences of frustration.
6. Discuss the social learning view of aggression.
7. Identify conditions that tend to provoke aggression.
8. Describe the effects of viewing pornography.
9. Describe television's effects on thinking and behaviour.
10. Discuss ways of reducing aggression.

CHAPTER REVIEW

Supply the words necessary to complete each of the following statements.

WHAT IS AGGRESSION?

1. Aggression is physical or verbal behaviour intended to _____
   someone. _____ aggression springs from anger and aims to injure.
   _____ aggression also aims to hurt but only as a means to an end.

THEORIES OF AGGRESSION

2. Sigmund Freud argued that aggression has its basis in a primitive death
   _____ that is redirected toward others. Konrad Lorenz also proposed a
   theory of inborn aggression but saw aggression as _____ rather than self-
   destructive. Both Freud and Lorenz agreed that aggressive energy is
   _____ and if it is not discharged it builds up until it
   _____.

3. Although the evidence does not support the instinct view, research has identified
   _____ influences upon aggression including _____, and
   blood _____.

4. A second theory, proposed by John Dollard and his associates in 1939, is that _____, or the blocking of goal-directed behaviour, invariably leads to aggression. Testing of this theory has produced mixed results: sometimes frustration leads to increased _____, sometimes not.

5. Frustration is created by a gap between our _____ and our attainments. Frustration is compounded when we compare ourselves to others. If we believe that others are better off than we are, we experience _____ deprivation.

6. _____ learning theory presents aggression as learned behaviour. Through experience and by _____ aggressive models, we learn that aggression often pays. Albert Bandura contends that aggressive acts are most likely when we are _____ by aversive experiences and it seems safe and _____ to aggress.

INFLUENCES ON AGGRESSION

7. Animals' reactions to shock indicate that _____ may provoke aggressive acts. Temporary climate variations affect one's behaviour, and _____ has been shown to increase aggression. Being _____ by another and crowding are also conducive to aggression.

8. Research indicates that our experience of emotion depends on how we _____ our bodily states. Thus arousal from almost any source, even physical _____ or sexual stimulation, combined with _____ thoughts and feelings can lead to aggression.

9. Leonard Berkowitz states that violence is most likely in the presence of _____ cues such as _____, which put physical and psychological _____ between the aggressor and the victim.

10. Recent studies indicate that viewing pornography distorts _____ of sexual reality, and may contribute to men's _____ toward women. Rather than advocate censorship, many psychologists favor "_____ _____ training."

11. The _____ hypothesis suggests that viewing violent drama enables people to release pent-up hostility. Research indicates that viewing violence produces an _____ in aggressive behaviour. It seems also to _____ viewers to aggression and to alter their _____ of reality. Television's greatest effect may be indirect as it _____ other activities.

12. Circumstances that provoke individuals to aggress can provoke _____ to do likewise. In fact, social interaction can actually _____ the aggressive reactions of individuals.

REDUCING AGGRESSION

13. The catharsis hypothesis, which predicts that the aggressive drive will be _____ after releasing aggressive energy, has not been confirmed. In some experiments aggressing has actually led to _____ aggression.

14. Social learning theory proposes we reduce aggression by modeling and _____ cooperative, nonaggressive behaviour. _____ is considerably less effective because it provides aversive stimulation and models the very behaviour it seeks to prevent. Since aggression is increased in the presence of aggressive cues, limiting the availability of _____ can reduce violence.

MATCHING TERMS

Write the letter of the correct term from the right before the appropriate number on the left.

_____ 1.   Redirecting aggression to a safer target.

_____ 2.   The blocking of goal-directed behaviour.

_____ 3.   Innate, unlearned behaviour exhibited by all members of a species.

_____ 4.   Stated that frustration produces aggression.

_____ 5.   It springs from anger and its goal is to injure.

_____ 6.   Something unpleasant or discomforting that can result in aggression.

_____ 7.   Anything that is perceived as an instrument of violence.

_____ 8.   A perspective that emphasizes the importance of observing and imitating others.

_____ 9.   It aims to hurt but only as a means to some other end.

_____ 10. The feeling of not having enough space.

_____ 11. Stated that a primitive death urge accounts for aggression.

_____ 12. Our perception that we are worse off compared to others.

_____ 13. Believes that individuals learn aggression from family, subcultures and media.

_____ 14. Emotional release.

a.   hostile aggression

b.   aggression cue

c.   relative deprivation

d.   catharsis

e.   displacement

f.   crowding

g.   aversive experience

h.   social learning theory

i.   frustration

j.   Dollard

k.   Freud

l.   Bandura

m.   instinctive behaviour

n.   instrumental aggression

TRUE-FALSE REVIEW

Circle T if the statement is true and F if it is false.

T F 1. Aggression is any behaviour that results in harm coming to another person.

T F 2. Hostile aggression seeks to injure but only as a means to some other end.

T F 3. All psychologists agree that aggression is maladaptive and self-destructive.

T F 4. Sigmund Freud theorized that human nature has within it a primitive death urge.

T F 5. Animals of many species have been bred for aggressiveness.

T F 6. Violent people are more likely to consume alcohol and to become aggressive when intoxicated.

T F 7. Half of identical twins of convicted criminals also have criminal records.

T F 8. In 1993, the murderer and/or the victim had been drinking in 65 percent of the homicides in the U.S.

T F 9. High levels of serotonin are often found among violence-prone children and adults.

T F 10. Frustration always results in some form of aggression.

T F 11. Revolutions of rising expectations indicate that those who are the most deprived are also those most frustrated.

T F 12. The term "relative deprivation" refers to the tendency to adapt to a lower level of stimulation.

T F 13. Social learning theory denies that frustration plays any role in aggression.

T F 14. Most abused children eventually become abusive parents.

T F 15. Research indicates that 70 percent of juveniles in detention did not grow up with two parents.

T F 16. Research has indicated that violent acts are more likely to occur on hot days.

T F 17. When countries adopt a law restricting handgun possession, the number of gun-related murders and suicides drop.

T F 18. Watching pornography has been proven to be a cause of rape.

T F 19. Half of the respondents in one survey of university women report having suffered some form of sexual assault on a date.

T F 20. The catharsis hypothesis assumes that aggression is produced by frustration.

T F 21. In one survey of prison inmates, 4 out of 10 said they had attempted specific crimes they had seen on television.

T F 22. Correlational studies but not laboratory experiments indicate that viewing aggression leads to aggression.

T F 23. Viewing television can mold our conceptions of the real world.

T F 24. After a war, a nation's murder rate tends to jump.

T F 25. Reward for nonaggression is more effective than punishment for aggression in reducing violence.

MULTIPLE-CHOICE PRACTICE TEST

Circle the correct letter.

1. According to the text, aggression always
   a. causes physical pain
   b. involves intent to harm someone
   c. involves emotional arousal
   d. is committed by someone who has been deliberately provoked

2. The murders committed by mobster "hit men" provide an example of
   a. emotional aggression
   b. silent aggression
   c. how catharsis can reduce aggression
   d. instrumental aggression

3. Which of the following would be an example of aggression as defined in the text?
   a. a wife deliberately belittles her husband in front of friends after he burns the pot roast
   b. a golfer accidentally hits another player with a golf ball
   c. a nurse gives a penicillin shot to a child
   d. a salesman tops his previous record by selling 50 cars in one month

4. Which of the following is the best example of instrumental aggression?
   a. an angry football player tackles a quarterback after he has completed a long pass
   b. a jealous wife finds her husband with another woman and shoots both of them
   c. a group of former soldiers kill the dictator of a small country for $10,000
   d. a man smashes his television set after he finds it does not work

5. In contrast to Freud's view of aggression, Lorenz
   a. supports the social learning explanation for aggression
   b. views aggression as instinctive
   c. views aggression as adaptive rather than destructive
   d. does not believe we have innate mechanisms for inhibiting aggression

6. What criticism has been leveled against instinct theory as an explanation for human aggression?
   a. it is an example of naming social behaviour but not explaining it
   b. research has indicated no clear biological influences on aggression
   c. it necessarily implies that aggression is adaptive
   d. it misinterprets correlation as evidence for causation

7. Research on biological influences on aggression indicates that
    a. animals of many species can be bred for aggressiveness
    b. neural influences facilitate animal aggression but not human aggression
    c. human aggression is instinctive
    d. there are no biochemical influences on aggression in humans

8. Which of the following is false?
    a. animals' "social" aggression and "silent" aggression seem to involve the same brain region
    b. alcohol enhances violence by reducing people's self-awareness
    c. low levels of serotonin are often found in the violence-prone
    d. "hostile" aggression springs from emotions such as anger

9. People who consume alcohol are
    a. better able to consider consequences of their actions
    b. more likely to be mellow rather than aggressive
    c. less self-aware, thus more likely to be violent
    d. more likely to have high levels of testosterone

10. Compared to prisoners convicted of nonviolent crimes, those convicted of unprovoked violent crimes tend to
    a. be first-borns
    b. have authoritarian attitudes
    c. be older
    d. have higher testosterone levels

11. A person kicking a dog after losing a game of checkers is an example of
    a. regression
    b. displacement
    c. relative frustration
    d. the weapons effect

12. Which of the following would be most frustrating?
    a. You only received a mark of 65 on the social psychology quiz.
    b. You were kept waiting for one hour at the doctor's office because the doctor had an emergency.
    c. You and a friend were both hired by the same company at the same time as computer programmers. Last week, your friend was given a raise but you weren't.
    d. Your friend walked right by you without saying "Hi".

13. _____ is a good predictor of perceived inequities by minority groups in Canada.
    a. Relative deprivation
    b. An aversive experience
    c. The amount of money people make
    d. Frustration which leads to aggression

14. To know whether people are frustrated we need to know
    a. their expectations and their attainments
    b. their level of deprivation and their power
    c. their wants and their intelligence
    d. their needs and their age

15. One principle which helps to explain people's rising expectations and therefore their continuing frustrations is
    a. displacement
    b. the hydraulic model
    c. aversive arousal
    d. relative deprivation

16. John has just received a 5 percent increase in salary. However, after learning that his coworkers have all received 10 percent increases, John becomes angry with his employer. We can understand John's feelings in terms of
    a. relative deprivation
    b. displacement
    c. aversive experience
    d. the hydraulic model of aggression

17. According to Bandura, a social learning theorist,
    a. frustration plays no role in aggression
    b. observing aggressive models promotes aggression
    c. the hydraulic model offers the best explanation for aggression
    d. hostile aggression is instinctive and instrumental aggression is learned

18. Research by Nisbett & Cohen (1996) found that white Southerners in the U. S. are more likely to advocate
    a. violence that protects one's health and home
    b. all forms of violence
    c. stricter gun control legislation
    d. media awareness training

19. Emotional arousal plus anticipated consequences provides the formula for aggression according to
    a. ethological theory
    b. catharsis theory
    c. frustration-aggression theory
    d. social learning theory

20. In studying the capacity of electric shock to elicit attack behaviour in rats, Nathan Azrin and his colleagues found that
    a. the shocked animals were choosy about their attack targets and would only attack other animals of the same species
    b. increasing the shock resulted in attempts on the part of the rats to escape rather than to attack
    c. the shock-attack reaction was clearly present in many different species
    d. shocks alone and not other aversive stimuli elicited attack

21. Which of the following is false?
    a. pain heightens aggressiveness in animals but not in humans
    b. being insulted by another is conducive to aggression
    c. in laboratory experiments heat triggers retaliative actions
    d. according to social learning theory, aggression is most likely when we are aroused and it seems safe and rewarding to aggress

22. Living three to a room in a college dorm seems to
    a. diminish one's sense of control
    b. lead to the establishment of stronger friendships
    c. lead to more hostile but less instrumental aggression
    d. improve grades because students are more likely to study in the library

23. In the Schacter and Singer experiment, which subjects felt the most anger?
    a. those who were given an adrenaline injection, were forewarned of the drug's effects, and were in the company of a euphoric person
    b. those who were given an adrenaline injection, were not forewarned of the drug's effects, and were in the company of a euphoric person
    c. those who were given an adrenaline injection, were forewarned of the drug's effects, and were in the company of a hostile person
    d. those who were given an adrenaline injection, were not forewarned of the drug's effects, and were in the company of a hostile person

24. According to the text, the fact that people from Hong Kong feel more fearful on their city streets that do people from Toronto may be due to the fact that Hong Kong
    a. has a higher average temperature
    b. has a lower per capita income
    c. has a higher crime rate
    d. is more densely populated

25. In a revision of frustration-aggression theory, Berkowitz theorized that
    a. frustration produces escape more often than aggression
    b. aggression is learned through a modeling effect
    c. aggression cues can release bottled-up anger
    d. frustration is instinctive

26. The text suggests that one reason Vancouver, British Columbia, has a 40 percent lower overall murder rate than Seattle, Washington, is because Vancouver
    a. has a lower average temperature
    b. has a lower unemployment rate
    c. restricts handgun ownership
    d. has a less congested population

27. Violent pornographic films often convey a false impression that
    a. women enjoy aggressive sexual encounters
    b. women are more likely to be rape victims than are men
    c. most rapes are never reported to the police
    d. most rapes are committed by victims' dates or acquaintances

28. Correlational research indicates that as pornography has become more widely available, the rate of reported rape has
    a. increased
    b. decreased
    c. remained unchanged
    d. increased in the short run but decreased in the long run

29. Sales rates of sexually explicit magazines such as <u>Hustler</u> and <u>Playboy</u> were positively correlated with state
    a. rape rates
    b. unemployment rates
    c. divorce rates
    d. child abuse rates

30. Research on rape in Canada, suggests that
    a. nine in 10 stranger rapes are not reported to police
    b. at least 20 percent of women surveyed reported an experience that met the legal definition of rape or attempted rape
    c. today's young women are less likely to report having been raped than are older women
    d. the rape rate is the lowest of most other industrialized countries

31. When university males have been asked whether there was any chance they would rape a woman "if you could be assured that no one would know and that you could in no way be punished," about _____ admit to at least a slim possibility of doing so.
    a. 1 in 20
    b. 1 in 10
    c. 1 in 5
    d. 1 in 3

32. As part of therapy, a clinical psychologist encourages her patients to install a punching bag in their homes to release hostility. The therapist apparently believes in
    a. social learning theory
    b. displacement
    c. the catharsis hypothesis
    d. aggressive physical exercise

33. In examining the relationship between viewing violence and aggressiveness in boys, Eron and Huesmann found that
    a. the viewing of violence at age eight was negatively correlated with aggressiveness at age nineteen
    b. the viewing of violence at age eight was positively correlated with aggressiveness at age nineteen
    c. aggressiveness at age eight was positively correlated with the viewing of violence at age nineteen
    d. both b and c are true

34. Research on the effects of televised violence indicates that
    a. viewing violence produces a modest increase in aggression
    b. viewing violence produces catharsis and thus a reduction in aggression
    c. there is no relationship between viewing aggression and behaving aggressively
    d. viewing violence increases aggression in adolescents but not in children

35. Research indicates that in comparison to light viewers, heavy viewers of television
    a. engage in greater prosocial behaviour
    b. underestimate the number of murders that occur annually in the United States
    c. think the world is a more dangerous place
    d. tend to be more extraverted

36. According to the author of the text, television's biggest effect may be that it
    a. desensitizes people to violence around them
    b. is the major cause of social violence
    c. presents an unreal picture of the world
    d. replaces other activities that people might engage in

37. University men who were angered by a fellow student retaliated with much stronger shock
    a. when in groups than when alone
    b. when the experimenter was not present than when he was observing their aggression
    c. when the subject was an acquaintance than when he was a stranger
    d. if after being angered, but before delivering shock, they were exposed to mildly erotic stimuli

38. Which of the following is true of findings regarding the catharsis hypothesis?
    a. catharsis never occurs
    b. the calming effect of retaliation seems to occur only in very specific circumstances
    c. the catharsis hypothesis has been well-supported
    d. the catharsis hypothesis is valid for adults but not for children

39. According to the text, the statement to a friend, "When you talk like that I feel irritated,"
    a. is, by definition, an act of angry aggression
    b. is best unsaid for it will prove frustrating to the friend and invite retaliation
    c. provides an informative, nonaggressive expression of feeling
    d. is best unsaid for while it may prove cathartic for you in the short run, it will make you feel more aggressive in the long run

40. Which of the following is probably least effective in reducing aggression?
    a. rewards for nonaggressive behaviour
    b. reducing the availability of weapons
    c. ignoring aggressive behaviour
    d. punishing aggressive behaviour

SHORT ESSAY QUESTIONS

Answer the following questions in the space provided.

1. State the difference between hostile and instrumental aggression.

2. Discuss how aggression is biologically influenced.

3. Give an example of relative deprivation from your own life.

4. Briefly describe the social learning view of aggression.

5. Describe three aversive experiences that may heighten aggression.

6. Explain how any form of emotional arousal can produce anger.

7. List two effects of viewing pornography.

8. Describe the effects of television's portrayal of violence.

9. List three effective ways of reducing aggression.

ANSWER KEY

Chapter Review

1. hurt
   Hostile
   Instrumental

2. urge
   adaptive
   instinctual
   explodes

3. biological
   heredity p330
   chemistry

4. frustration
   aggressiveness

5. expectations
   relative

6. Social
   observing
   aroused
   rewarding

7. pain
   heat
   attacked

8. interpret
   exercise
   hostile

9. aggressive
   guns
   distance

10. perceptions
    aggression
    media awareness

11. catharsis
    increase
    desensitize
    perceptions
    replaces

12. groups
    amplify

13. drained
    heightened

14. rewarding
    Punishment
    weapons

Matching Terms

1. e
2. i
3. m
4. j
5. a
6. g
7. b
8. h
9. n
10. f
11. k
12. c
13. l
14. d

True-False Review

1. F
2. F
3. F
4. T
5. T
6. T
7. T
8. T
9. F
10. F
11. F
12. F
13. F
14. F
15. T
16. T
17. T
18. F
19. T
20. F

21. T
22. F
23. T

24. T
25. T

Multiple-Choice Practice Test

1. b
2. d
3. a
4. c
5. c
6. a
7. a
8. a
9. c
10. d
11. b
12. c
13. a
14. a
15. d
16. a
17. b
18. a
19. d
20. c

21. a
22. a
23. d
24. d
25. c
26. c
27. a
28. a
29. a
30. b
31. d
32. c
33. b
34. a
35. c
36. d
37. a
38. b
39. c
40. d

CHAPTER 11
ATTRACTION AND INTIMACY: LIKING AND LOVING OTHERS

CHAPTER OBJECTIVES

After completing your study of this chapter you should be able to:

1. Discuss the role of proximity and physical attractiveness in initial attraction.
2. Analyze research findings on the role of similarity in friendship.
3. Explain why liking is usually mutual.
4. Explain the reward theory of attraction.
5. Describe the nature and theory of passionate love and identify cultural, personality, and gender variations in love.
6. Discuss the nature of companionate love.
7. Identify the different attachment styles that characterize interpersonal relationships.
8. Discuss the importance of equity and self-disclosure in close relationships.
9. Identify several predictors of a stable marriage.
10. Describe the detachment process.

CHAPTER REVIEW

Supply the words necessary to complete each of the following statements.

1. We have an intense need to _____, that is, to connect to others in enduring close relationships. When this need is thwarted by _____, we feel ignored, _____, and anxious; our work is _____ and our life is unsettled.

BONDING: FORMING RELATIONSHIPS

2. A powerful predictor of whether any two people are friends is their sheer _____ to one another. It provides people with the opportunity for _____ and thus to discover their similarities and to feel one another's liking. Even the _____ of interacting with another can boost liking. Research also indicates that mere repeated _____ tends to increase attraction.

3. A second determinant of one's initial liking for another is physical _____. Evolutionary psychologists maintain that natural selection explains males' greater _____ initiative and physical _____. Generally, women prefer men who possess external _____ and can offer physical protection. Men, however, are attracted to women whose physical features suggest _____.

4. The _____ phenomenon is the tendency for people to pair off with others who are about as attractive as themselves. Research indicates the presence of a strong physical-attractiveness _____: the assumption that what is beautiful is _____.

5. Acquaintances are likely to develop a friendship if there is _____ of beliefs, attitudes, and values. Little support has been found for the _____ hypothesis which proposes that we are attracted to those whose needs are different from our own. Apparently _____ rarely attract.

6. We are also likely to develop friendships with people who _____ us. This is particularly true when we do not attribute the other's flattery to some ingratiating motive, when we have recently been deprived of _____, and when the other's praise _____ earlier criticism.

7. We like those who _____ us or those who are associated with _____ feelings.

LOVE

8. _____ love is a state of intense longing for union with another. Such love often includes elation and gloom, exhilaration and misery.

9. The two-factor theory of emotion states that arousal x _____ = emotion. Thus any arousal can intensify passionate feelings provided one can attribute some of the arousal to a _____ stimulus.

10. Although all cultures have a concept of _____ love, they differ in their belief that love is a precondition for marriage. Studies of men and women have also found that it is _____ who tend to fall in love more readily.

11. _____ love is the affection we feel for those with whom our lives are deeply intertwined. Such love thrives where a relationship is _____ and mutually rewarding.

MAINTAINING CLOSE RELATIONSHIPS

12. From infancy to old age, _____ are central to human life. In terms of specific styles, _____ individuals find it easy to get close to others. _____ individuals may fear closeness or want to feel self-sufficient. _____-ambivalent individuals are less trusting, and thus more possessive and jealous.

13. We exchange rewards by an _____ principle. It states that what people receive from a relationship should be _____ to what they contribute to it. Tit-for-tat exchanges seem to increase people's liking for one another when their relationship is relatively _____ but diminish liking when the two seek true _____. Still, relationships are likely to endure when both partners feel it to be equitable.

14. Intimacy is fostered by reciprocal _____ in which we drop our masks and gradually let ourselves be known as we are. Couples who most reveal themselves to one another tend to express _____ satisfaction with their relationship and thus it is more likely to_____.

ENDING RELATIONSHIPS

15. Divorce risk is lower for those who marry after age _____, are well-_____, and are _____ committed. As an alternative to divorce, some people cope with a failing relationship by exhibiting _____, optimistically waiting for conditions to improve. Others passively allow the relationship to deteriorate. Still others _____ their concerns and take active steps to improve the relationship.

MATCHING TERMS

Write the letter of the correct term from the right before the appropriate number on the left.

_____ 1.   A strategy to gain another's favor.

_____ 2.   A need to connect with others in enduring close relationships.

_____ 3.   Stimuli are rated more positively after being shown repeatedly.

_____ 4.   Liking those who are associated with good feelings.

_____ 5.   What is beautiful is good.

_____ 6.   This fosters intimacy.

_____ 7.   Outcomes are in proportion to inputs.

_____ 8.   The affection we feel for those with whom our lives are deeply intertwined.

_____ 9.   One of the most powerful predictors of whether two people are friends.

_____ 10. People choose partners who are about as attractive as themselves.

_____ 11. "Intense longing for union with another."

_____ 12. People attract those whose needs are different, in ways that complement their own.

a. equity

b. proximity

c. mere-exposure effect

d. physical-attractiveness stereotype

e. matching phenomenon

f. complementarity hypothesis

g. ingratiation

h. reward principle

i. passionate love

j. self-disclosure

k. companionate love

l. need to belong

TRUE-FALSE REVIEW

Circle T if the statement is true and F if it is false.

T F 1. All cultures use ostracism to control people's behaviour.

T F 2. Cognitive dissonance theory provides the most popular theory of social attraction.

T F 3. One of the most powerful predictors of whether any two people are friends is their sheer proximity to one another.

T F 4. Merely anticipating that we will interact with someone increases liking of that person.

T F 5. Novel stimuli are rated more negatively after being shown repeatedly.

T F 6. Evolutionary psychologists say men seek to produce widely, women wisely.

T F 7. Men are more prone to sexual jealousy than women.

T F 8. Women more than men worry about their physical appearance and constitute 90 percent of cosmetic surgery patients.

T F 9. Physically attractive men and women tend to be looked on by others as colder, dumber, and less moral than plainer people.

T F 10. Women tend to be judged as more physically attractive if they have "baby-face" features that suggest nondominance.

T F 11. Across the world people show little agreement about the features of an ideal male or female face.

T F 12. A 17-year-old girl's facial attractiveness is a weak predictor of her attractiveness at age 30.

T F 13. Evidence strongly supports the complementarity hypothesis.

T F 14. The happiest couples are those who idealize one another, even seeing their partners more positively than their partners see themselves.

T F 15.   We are more attracted to someone who likes us from the start than to someone who likes us after initially disliking us.

T F 16.   University students who evaluated strangers in a pleasant room liked them better than did those who did their evaluations in an uncomfortably hot room.

T F 17.   The two-factor theory of emotion states that love is a product of jealousy and ecstasy.

T F 18.   Most cultures do not have a concept of romantic love.

T F 19.   Men are more likely than women to initiate the breakup of a premarital romance.

T F 20.   Only 4 in 10 infants exhibit secure attachment.

T F 21.   Equity is a condition in which people receive equal outcomes from a relationship.

T F 22.   One experiment found that tit-for-tat exchanges actually diminished liking when two people sought true friendship.

T F 23.   Researchers have found that women are often more willing to disclose their fears and weaknesses than are men.

T F 24.   Individualistic cultures have higher divorce rates than collectivist cultures.

T F 25.   Months or years later, people recall more pain over spurning someone's love than over having been spurned.

MULTIPLE-CHOICE PRACTICE TEST

Circle the correct letter.

1. The need to belong and to form close interpersonal relationships
   a. is at the core of our existence and thus is characteristic of people everywhere
   b. is largely a 20th century motive that is most evident in industrialized societies
   c. is a learned motive serving our more fundamental need for self-esteem
   d. encourages ostracism of others

2. Tom, who tends to be extraverted, has just moved into the dormitory at Federal College. He is most likely to make friends with
   a. Bill, his next-door neighbor
   b. John, a chemistry major who lives across campus
   c. Michael, an introvert who lives on the next floor
   d. Stuart, a student who lives off campus and who loves dogs

3. When identical twins were asked their reactions to their co-twin's selection of a marriage partner, _____ percent said, "I could have fallen for my twin's fiancée."
   a. 95
   b. 65
   c. 35
   d. 5

4. Which of the following is supported by the research on social attraction?
   a. familiarity breeds fondness
   b. opposites attract
   c. beauty times brains equals a constant
   d. absence makes the heart grow fonder

5. The mere-exposure effect provides one possible explanation for
   a. why proximity leads to liking
   b. why similarity leads to liking
   c. the equity phenomenon
   d. the matching phenomenon

6. French students' least favorite letter among the letters of the alphabet is
   a. the least frequent letter in the French language
   b. the hardest letter to draw
   c. the last letter of the alphabet
   d. the hardest letter to pronounce

7. Some years ago, a mysterious student enveloped in a big, black bag began attending a speech class at a state university. While the teacher knew the "Black Bag's" identity, the other students did not. As the semester progressed, the students' attitude toward the Black Bag changed from hostility to curiosity to friendship. What may best explain the students' change in attitude?
    a. exposure breeds liking
    b. stress produces affiliation
    c. boredom breeds a liking for the novel
    d. similarity attracts

8. A stranger rides the same bus you do to school every day. According to the "mere-exposure effect," as the days pass you will come to view the stranger
    a. as merely another student
    b. more unfavorably
    c. more critically
    d. more favorably

9. The evolutionary perspective suggests that females are most attracted to males who show
    a. empathy, nurturance, and self-sacrifice
    b. similarity in beliefs, attitudes, and values
    c. an ability to provide and protect resources
    d. high self-esteem, extroversion, and self-efficacy

10. Based on research presented in the text, if you go out on a blind date you would be most influenced by your date's
    a. open-mindedness
    b. sense of humor
    c. physical attractiveness
    d. sincerity

11. The finding that people pair off with others who are about as attractive as themselves is known as
    a. the matching phenomenon
    b. complementarity
    c. the reciprocity effect
    d. Gause's law

12. Mary, who is attractive, very intelligent, and high in social status marries Tom who is also attractive, very intelligent, and high in social status. Their relationship is best understood as an example of
    a. the ingratiation effect
    b. complementarity
    c. the mere-exposure effect
    d. the matching phenomenon

13. Which of the following seems to be true from research on social attraction?
    a. what is beautiful is judged to be good
    b. what is familiar is judged to be boring
    c. what is unique is judged to be valuable
    d. what is average is judged to be unattractive

14. Research indicates that we judge beautiful people to be more
    a. manipulative
    b. honest
    c. concerned for others
    d. intelligent

15. According to the text, differences in the psychological characteristics of attractive and unattractive people are
    a. innate
    b. in the eye of the beholder and really do not exist
    c. the result of self-fulfilling prophecies
    d. an example of how the researcher's values may determine the outcome of research

16. When shown a picture of an average young woman, men who had been watching three beautiful women on television's Charlie's Angels rated her as _____ than did men who had not been watching the program.
    a. more attractive
    b. less attractive
    c. more intelligent
    d. less intelligent

17. Research by John Lydon and his colleagues (1999) has found that when people who are in a highly committed relationship encounter an attractive member of the opposite sex, they see this person as
    a. less attractive unless the person is interested in meeting them
    b. less attractive but only when the person is interested in meeting them
    c. more attractive unless the person is interested in meeting them
    d. more attractive but only when the person is interested in meeting them

18. George is a white student who has been given the choice to work on a project with either John or Bob. John is a black student who shares similar attitudes and work ethics as George. Bob is a white student who seems very different from George. Who will George be more likely to choose to work with?
    a. John
    b. Bob
    c. George will like both John and Bob equally well
    d. George will not like John and Bob equally

19. The idea that we are attracted to people who are in some ways different from ourselves is an essential aspect of the
    a. companionate love hypothesis
    b. matching phenomenon
    c. complementarity hypothesis
    d. reward theory of attraction

20. Mary, a talkative, extraverted, young woman, is strongly attracted to Ronald, a quiet, introverted, middle-aged man. Mary's attraction to Ronald would be best explained by
    a. exchange theory
    b. the matching phenomenon
    c. the equity principle
    d. the complementarity hypothesis

21. People who were asked to rank _____ reasons for going out with their boyfriend or girlfriend later expressed less love for their partner than did people who were asked to rank _____ reasons.
    a. companionate, romantic
    b. extrinsic, intrinsic
    c. intrinsic, extrinsic
    d. common, unique

22. You overhear a casual acquaintance express approval of you in the coffee shop. You are most likely to think well of that acquaintance if
    a. you had learned an hour earlier that you had received an average grade on a history test
    b. you had learned an hour earlier that you had failed a chemistry test
    c. the acquaintance is unattractive
    d. the acquaintance is engaged to be married

23. Research suggests we may be most attracted to the person who
    a. has always said only positive things about us
    b. once said negative things about us but now evaluates us positively
    c. once said positive things but now evaluates us negatively
    d. generally says negative things about us but occasionally says something positive

24. Research by Murray and Holmes (1997) finds that when people have positive illusions about their partners they
    a. are at risk to break up
    b. tend to treat their partners harshly when they do not meet their expectations
    c. tend to engage in upward social comparisons with their peers
    d. become more satisfied with their relationships over time

25. Reward theory states that
    a. rewards foster romantic but not companionate love
    b. companionate love is fostered by long periods of separation
    c. flattery always leads to increased liking
    d. we like those people who are associated with good feelings

26. Research o Robert Sternberg views love as a triangle whose three sides include all of the following except
    a. friendship
    b. commitment
    c. intimacy
    d. passion

27. According to the two-factor theory, emotion is a result of
    a. motives and thoughts
    b. rewards and punishments
    c. nature and nurture
    d. arousal and a label

28. The concept of romantic love is present
    a. only in individualistic societies
    b. only in affluent societies
    c. only in cultures where there are clear differences in gender roles
    d. in most cultures

29. Compared to men who were interviewed on a low, solid bridge, men interviewed on a narrow, wobbly bridge liked a
    a. female interviewer more
    b. male interviewer more
    c. female interviewer less
    d. male interviewer less

30. Studies of men and women falling in and out of love have revealed that men tend to
    a. fall more readily in love and more slowly out of love
    b. fall more readily in love and more readily out of love
    c. fall more slowly in love and more slowly out of love
    d. fall more slowly in love and more readily out of love

31. In a study of arranged versus love-based marriages in India, researchers found that
    a. love-based marriages were more likely to survive
    b. those in arranged marriages experienced reactance and never felt feelings of love for their spouse
    c. after five years of marriage, those in love-based marriages reported diminished feelings of love while those in arranged marriages reported more love
    d. those in love-based marriages were more likely to demonstrate the disclosure reciprocity effect

32. Compared to North Americans, Asians may be less vulnerable to disillusionment in love relationships because they
    a. are less susceptible to relative deprivation and to social comparison
    b. are more likely to substitute ludus for eros
    c. experience a greater variety of emotionally arousing situations that are steered into passionate love
    d. are less focused on personal feelings and more concerned with practical aspects of social attachments

33. In terms of adult attachment styles, _____ individuals seem to be possessive and jealous while _____ individuals are less invested in relationships and more likely to leave them.
    a. secure; insecure
    b. anxious-ambivalent; avoidance
    c. avoidance; anxious-ambivalent
    d. insecure; apathetic

34. Our desire to return a favor received from another is best explained in terms of the
    a. complementarity hypothesis
    b. equity rule
    c. matching phenomenon
    d. mere-exposure effect

35. Research on equity in interpersonal relationships suggests that
    a. a marriage contract is more likely to undermine than enhance the couple's love
    b. tit-for-tat exchanges decrease people's liking for one another in business relationships
    c. the principle is innate
    d. following the principle increases liking between males but decreases liking between females

36. An employee who feels underpaid may demand an increase in wages or exert less effort at his or her task. This behaviour is an
    a. attempt to restore equity
    b. attempt to achieve complementarity
    c. example of the matching phenomenon
    d. example of the overexposure effect

37. Which of the following is true of self-disclosure?
    a. disclosure begets disclosure
    b. a person who engages in self-disclosure is perceived as anxious
    c. a person who engages in self-disclosure is perceived as manipulative
    d. self-disclosure leads to infatuation but not to true love

38. Bill and Sara's relationship becomes progressively more intimate as each engages in a bit more self-revelation in response to the other's self-disclosure. Their relationship is marked by the _____ effect.
    a. disclosure reciprocity
    b. mutual disinhibition
    c. reciprocal disinhibition
    d. reciprocal intimacy

39. People seem to have a lower risk of divorce if they
    a. had parents who divorced
    b. live in a large town or city
    c. cohabited before marriage
    d. are religiously committed

40. Which of the following is true?
    a. companionate love typically leads to romantic love
    b. self-disclosure reduces feelings of romantic love
    c. companionate love is more likely to endure when both partners feel it to be equitable
    d. spouses who pray together are more likely to report conflict in their marriage

SHORT ESSAY QUESTIONS

Answer the following questions in the space provided.

1. Identify the 5 factors that influence liking and friendship.

2. Why does proximity promote friendship?

3. Explain the physical-attractiveness stereotype?

4. What is the complementarity hypothesis? What does research indicate regarding it?

5. Describe the reward theory of attraction.

6. How does the two-factor theory of emotion explain passionate love?

7. Compare and contrast passionate love with companionate love.

8. Explain the equity principle and discuss its relevance to friendship and love.

9. Discuss the causes and effects of self-disclosure.

10. Identify four factors that are associated with a lower risk of divorce.

ANSWER KEY

Chapter Review

1. belong
   ostracism
   depressed
   disrupted

2. proximity
   interaction
   anticipation
   exposure

3. attractiveness
   sexual
   aggression
   resources
   fertility

4. matching
   stereotype
   good

5. similarity
   complementarity
   opposites

6. like
   approval
   reverses

7. reward
   good

8. Passionate

9. label
   romantic

10. romantic
    men

11. companionate
    intimate

12. attachments
    secure
    Avoidance
    Anxious

13. equity
    proportional
    formal
    friendship

14. disclosure
    more
    endure

15. 20
    educated
    religiously
    loyalty
    voice

Matching Terms

1. g
2. l
3. c
4. h
5. d
6. j

7. a
8. k
9. b
10. e
11. i
12. f

True-False Review

1. T
2. F
3. T
4. T
5. F
6. T
7. T
8. T
9. F
10. T

11. F
12. T
13. F
14. T
15. F
16. T
17. F
18. F
19. F
20. F

21.	F		24.	T
22.	T		25.	T
23.	T			

Multiple-Choice Practice Test

1.	a		21.	b
2.	a		22.	b
3.	d		23.	b
4.	a		24.	d
5.	a		25.	d
6.	a		26.	a
7.	a		27.	d
8.	d		28.	d
9.	c		29.	a
10.	c		30.	a
11.	a		31.	c
12.	d		32.	d
13.	a		33.	b
14.	d		34.	b
15.	c		35.	a
16.	b		36.	a
17.	b		37.	a
18.	a		38.	a
19.	c		39.	d
20.	d		40.	c

CHAPTER 12
PREJUDICE: DISLIKING OTHERS

CHAPTER OBJECTIVES

After completing your study of this chapter you should be able to:

1. Distinguish between prejudice and discrimination.
2. Discuss the evidence for prejudice in Canada.
3. Analyze how unequal status and the formation of groups foster prejudice.
4. Demonstrate how prejudice is maintained through conformity.
5. Explain the dynamics of authoritarianism.
6. Explain the scapegoat theory of prejudice.
7. Describe how emotions influence feelings of prejudice.
8. Explain how stereotypes can be a by-product of our normal thinking processes.
9. Identify cognitive consequences of stereotypes.
10. Discuss how people react to prejudice.

CHAPTER REVIEW

Supply the words necessary to complete each of the following statements.

THE NATURE AND POWER OF PREJUDICE

1. Prejudice is a negative _____ of a group and its individual members. The beliefs supporting prejudice are called _____, and they are often inaccurate and resistant to new information.

2. Discrimination is unjustifiable negative _____ toward a group. The terms "racism" and "_____" refer to institutional practices that discriminate, even when there is no prejudicial intent.

3. Surveys suggest that overt expressions of _____ have decreased and that Canadians are motivated to develop a _____ society. While less blatant, prejudice exists in _____ forms as evidenced in experiments which evaluated people's actual _____ toward Blacks and Whites and as demonstrated by people's _____ reactions to isolated minority people.

4. Prejudice can be _____ (conscious) or _____ (automatic) which can trigger a knee-jerk _____.

SOCIAL SOURCES OF PREJUDICE

5. _____ status breeds prejudice as the group that enjoys superiority seeks to justify its standing. Realistic group _____ theory suggests that prejudice arises from competition for scarce _____.

6. We define ourselves by our groups. Experiments reveal that _____ bias may arise from merely dividing people into _____. Even when the us–them distinction is trivial, people may show _____ towards their own group and _____ towards an outgroup.

7. Once prejudice becomes a social norm, it is maintained partly through the inertia of _____.

8. _____ people believe their group is superior to all other groups. These _____ people are submissive to those in power and _____ to those deemed inferior. Such people tend to be prejudiced to all ethnic minorities.

EMOTIONAL SOURCES OF PREJUDICE

9. _____ often evokes hostility which may be vented on scapegoats. This phenomenon of "_____ aggression" may have contributed to lynchings of African Americans in the south whenever cotton prices were _____ and to the extermination of Jews during World War II.

10. Moods influence how we perceive others. Research indicates that when we are in a bad mood we evaluate others more _____. Sometimes _____ attitudes of other groups serve to keep the group in a lower social standing. Such _____ prejudice, often seen in attitudes towards women, can be a potent cause of _____.

COGNITIVE SOURCES OF PREJUDICE

11. The same thought processes that allow people to make sense of their world can lead people to make _____ evaluations of others. Once people are categorized into groups, we tend to perceive that they are "all alike", a concept called outgroup _____ effect. However we perceive our own _____ composed of diverse individuals.

12. _____ people draw our attention making us aware of differences we would otherwise not notice. We also better remember vivid cases and may use them to judge an entire _____. Our attentiveness to unusual occurrences can also create _____ correlations. For example, a minority person committing an unusual crime may lead us to associate such people with such behaviour.

13. _____ errors can bias people's explanations of group members. In the _____-_____ bias we explain away outgroup members' positive behaviours and attribute their negative behaviours to their dispositions. Blaming victims also results from believing we live in a _____ world where people get what they deserve.

14. By directing our attention, _____, and memories, stereotypes lead us to find supporting evidence, even when none exists. Stereotypes are self-_____, thus resistant to change. When people get to know an individual, they may set aside their stereotypes. Stereotypes are more potent when judging _____ individuals and when deciding policies regarding entire groups. Stereotypes can subtly color our assessments of individuals' behaviours, as when assertive behaviour is evaluated more _____ if coming from a woman.

REACTIONS TO PREJUDICE AND STEREOTYPING

15. People who experience discrimination can feel a loss of _____ over their environment. They generally feel anxious and _____. Victims protect their self-_____ by attributing the negative evaluations they face to _____.

16. Prejudice can lead to negative performance through _____-_____ prophecies. If we believe that others expect us to perform poorly, our anxiety may cause us to _____ the belief — a phenomenon called the _____ threat.

17. Although _____ bias exists, most women _____ feeling personally discriminated against. They believe it is something that other women face. This personal/group discrimination _____ enables individuals to maintain a perception of _____ in their lives. Facing prejudice can make social interactions _____.

MATCHING TERMS

Write the letter of the correct term from the right before the appropriate number on the left.

_____ 1. Belief in the superiority of one's ethnic or cultural group.

_____ 2. Individuals' prejudicial attitudes and discriminatory behaviour toward people of a given sex.

_____ 3. Unjustifiable negative behaviour toward a group and its members.

_____ 4. Explaining away outgroup members positive behaviours while attributing negative behaviours to their dispositions.

_____ 5. Institutional practices that subordinate people of a given race.

_____ 6. Tending toward punitiveness and rigidity in thinking.

_____ 7. A negative prejudgment of a group and its members.

_____ 8. Forming a new stereotype of professional, middle-class Blacks."

_____ 9. People get what they deserve and deserve what they get.

_____ 10. Provides an explanation for the lynchings of African-Americans in the South.

_____ 11. A belief about the personal attributes of a group of people.

_____ 12. Concern that one will verify a stereotype.

_____ 13. Prejudice arises when groups compete for scarce resources.

_____ 14. Perceiving outgroup members as more similar to one another than are ingroup members.

a. outgroup homogeneity effect

b. realistic group conflict theory

c. authoritarianism

d. scapegoat theory

e. ethnocentrism

f. subtyping

g. stereotype threat

h. prejudice

i. discrimination

j. racism

k. stereotype

l. sexism

m. group-serving bias

n. belief in a just world

TRUE-FALSE REVIEW

Circle T if the statement is true and F if it is false.

T F 1.   Prejudice is unjustifiable negative behaviour toward a group and its members.

T F 2.   Acceptance of ethnic diversity and members of ethnic groups in Canada has increased in recent decades.

T F 3.   Racism refers not only to attitudes but also to behaviour and institutional practices that subordinate people of a given race.

T F 4.   Prejudice operates partly as an unconscious, unintended response.

T F 5.   Gender stereotypes help to rationalize gender roles.

T F 6.   Some research indicates that merely composing groups X and Y with a flip of the coin is sufficient to produce ingroup bias.

T F 7.   Ingroup bias results as much or more from perceiving that one's own group is good as from a sense that other groups are bad.

T F 8.   People whose positive self-image is threatened tend to be more prejudiced.

T F 9.   Children of employed women have less stereotyped views of men and women.

T F 10. The authoritarian personality is prejudiced toward Blacks but not toward other minority groups.

T F 11. During the early 1900s when cotton crops were poor, White people went out of their way to be helpful to Black people.

T F 12. When people are in a good mood they are more likely to rate visible minorities negatively.

T F 13. Compared to nonprejudiced people, prejudiced people take less time to categorize others by race.

T F 14.   When White and Black students are shown faces of a few White and Black individuals and then asked to pick these individuals out of a photographic lineup, both White and Black students more accurately recognize the White faces than the Black.

T F 15.   Greater familiarity with a social group prevents us from seeing its diversity.

T F 16.   The term "group-serving bias" refers to negative judgments we make about individuals in our own family and circle of friends.

T F 17.   The need to believe in a just world provides an explanation for why we disparage victims of injustice.

T F 18.   People often evaluate individuals more positively than the groups they compose.

T F 19.   When students get good grades, female professors are judged more positively than their male counterparts.

T F 20.   We rely more heavily on stereotypes when dealing with people and situations that are unfamiliar.

T F 21.   Behaving in the way that is expected is an example of the self-fulfilling prophecy.

T F 22.   Positive stereotypes disrupt performance just as much as negative stereotypes.

T F 23.   Most women feel personally discriminated against.

T F 24.   People tend to report that they have experienced more discrimination than the typical members of their social group have.

T F 25.   Stigma conscious people expect others to view them negatively.

MULTIPLE-CHOICE PRACTICE TEST

Circle the correct letter.

1. Prejudice is a negative _____ while discrimination is negative
   _____.
   a. belief; feeling
   b. generalization; practice
   c. attitude; behaviour
   d. stereotype; practice

2. Stereotypes are to discrimination as _____ are to
   _____.
   a. categories; feelings
   b. attitudes; actions
   c. emotions; practice
   d. beliefs; behaviour

3. Mr. Watson's belief that Blacks are lazy is an example of _____.
   His refusal to rent an apartment to a Black family is an example of _____.
   a. a stereotype; sexism
   b. discrimination; prejudice
   c. a stereotype; discrimination
   d. racism; prejudice

4. Racism"
   a. can refer to institutional practices that discriminate even when there is no prejudicial
      intent
   b. refers to institutional practices that discriminate but only if there is prejudicial intent
   c. refers only to individuals' prejudicial attitudes
   d. refers only to individuals' discriminatory behaviour

5. Survey research on the acceptance of ethnic diversity in Canada indicates that the level of
   acceptance of minority groups
   a. has decreased in recent decades
   b. has remained the same for the last 50 years
   c. has increased in recent decades
   d. depends on the region of the country

6. Which of the following would be an example of racism as the term is defined in the text?
    a. Mr. Jones' refusal to rent his apartments to Chinese
    b. Mrs. Smith's prejudice toward Hispanics
    c. a government regulation that prevents inner-city residents from being recruited to serve as Army officers
    d. all of the above

7. Realistic group conflict theory suggests that prejudice arises
    a. where there is a long history of distrust between two groups
    b. when a new group moves into an area
    c. when groups fail to communicate clearly with each other
    d. when groups compete for scarce resources

8. The idea that we find it useful to put people, ourselves included, into categories is an important assumption of _____ theory.
    a. just world
    b. realistic group conflict
    c. social identity
    d. cognitive bias

9. The in-group bias seems to occur more frequently among
    a. females than among males
    b. the young than among the old
    c. people from individualistic cultures than among people from communal cultures
    d. Blacks than among Whites

10. Sam and Nathan play on different college soccer teams. When their teams play each other, Sam and Nathan each believe that their team is the better team. This illustrates
    a. outgroup homogeneity effect
    b. outgroup bias
    c. ingroup bias
    d. group-serving bias

11. A person whose self-esteem has been threatened (for example a student who does poorly on a test) is more likely to
    a. judge another student's work less harshly than his own
    b. judge another student's work more harshly than his own
    c. judge another student's work about the same as his own
    d. feel more positively about a person from another culture

12. In the 1950s, racial integration was accepted in Indiana steel mills and West Virginia coal mines. However, in the neighborhoods of those employed in the mills and mines, segregation was practiced. This is an example of how prejudice may be based in
    a. authoritarianism
    b. the just world phenomenon
    c. frustration
    d. conformity

13. Studies by Pettigrew of Whites in South Africa and the American South revealed that during the 1950s
    a. prejudice had its basis in competition for housing and jobs
    b. those who were prejudiced were authoritarian personalities
    c. prejudice was based in displaced aggression
    d. those who conformed most to other social norms were also most prejudiced

14. Which of the following is particularly characteristic of the authoritarian personality?
    a. being intolerant of weakness
    b. experiencing a happy childhood
    c. occupying a political office with considerable authority
    d. being an only child

15. Which of the following would you not expect to be true of the authoritarian personality?
    a. to discriminate against American Indians
    b. to want to achieve high social status
    c. to be respectful of police
    d. to be opposed to capital punishment

16. In repressive regimes across the world, people who become torturers tend to have
    a. low self-esteem
    b. authoritarian attitudes
    c. low intelligence
    d. a sense of external control

17. According to the text, the authoritarian personality is an example of
    a. how conformity supports prejudice
    b. a cognitive source of prejudice
    c. how emotional needs contribute to prejudice
    d. how social inequalities breed prejudice

18. Victoria Esses and Mark Zanna (1995) found that when people listened to music that put them in a bad mood they
   a. experienced catharsis when they made a positive evaluation of visible minorities
   b. made attributions that justified their actions
   c. evaluated all people negatively
   d. evaluated visible minorities negatively
   e.

19. The tendency after World War I, for Germans to see Jewish people as villains was cited in the text as evidence for
   a. the belief in a just world
   b. the ultimate attribution error
   c. the scapegoat theory
   d. outgroup homogeneity effect

20. John has just failed a chemistry test. He goes back to his apartment and criticizes his roommate's choice of music. What term best describes John's behaviour?
   a. institutionalized aggression
   b. just world action
   c. displaced aggression
   d. authoritarian regression

21. Which of the following is an example of benevolent sexism?
   a. women are much more helpful than men
   b. women are less competitive than men
   c. once married, women put their husbands on a tight rein
   d. all of the above

22. Research investigating the effects of moods on stereotyping indicates that
   a. bad moods amplify outgroup stereotyping while good moods decrease it
   b. positive emotions improve complex thinking and thus the ability to see individual differences
   c. bad moods lead to more introspective thinking and thus less stereotyping
   d. feeling really good may prime feelings of superiority

23. The statement, "They are all alike and different from us" reflects
   a. ingroup bias
   b. outgroup bias
   c. outgroup homogeneity effect
   d. categorization effect

24. The stereotype of _____ is held by both men and women, by both feminists and nonfeminists.
    a. men as leaders
    b. men as decision makers
    c. women as homemakers
    d. women as mediators

25. Which of the following is true?
    a. pervasive gender stereotypes continue to exist
    b. prejudice against women has not declined in the last 15 years
    c. racial stereotypes are stronger than gender stereotypes
    d. stereotypes are the same as prejudices

26. Students were told the actions of 50 men, 10 of whom had performed either nonviolent crimes or violent crimes. When later asked to make judgments about the men,
    a. the subjects shown the list with the violent crimes most overestimated the number of criminal acts
    b. the subjects shown the list with the nonviolent crimes most overestimated the number of criminal acts
    c. the subjects judged all the men to be members of outgroups
    d. male subjects made more accurate judgments about the number of criminal acts than did female subjects

27. The co-occurrence of two distinctive events can create
    a. belief in a just world
    b. illusory correlation
    c. illusion of control
    d. the ultimate attribution error

28. In one study, students were told that various members of "Group A" or "Group B" did either something desirable or something undesirable. While many more statements described members of Group A than Group B, both groups were associated with nine desirable behaviours for every four undesirable behaviours. Results indicated
    a. that students perceived members of Group B more negatively
    b. that students perceived members of Group A more negatively
    c. no differences in the students' perceptions of the groups
    d. that "authoritarian" students viewed Group A more negatively

29. The group-serving bias seems to be less characteristic of
    a. individualistic groups
    b. groups that stress honesty
    c. disadvantaged groups
    d. collectivist groups

30. Explaining away outgroup members' positive behaviours and attributing negative behaviours to their dispositions is referred to as
    a. the outgroup homogeneity effect
    b. group-serving bias
    c. the just world phenomenon
    d. the scapegoat theory of prejudice

31. Which of the following would be an example of the "group-serving bias"?
    a. Vera believes that women are unemployed because of discrimination while men are unemployed because of low motivation
    b. Sue believes that members of her own family are prejudiced while her husband's family is tolerant
    c. Chuck believes that mistakes made by both men and women are due to low intelligence
    d. Bill believes that groups outperform individuals in solving problems

32. According to Lerner, our need to believe in a just world often leads us to blame
    a. fate
    b. supernatural forces
    c. the social structure
    d. the victim

33. A belief in a just world may lead us to believe that an unemployed person is
    a. a victim of discrimination
    b. lazy
    c. in need of sympathy
    d. in need of a retraining program

34. The results of one social-psychological study indicated that observers who discovered that a fellow worker had received a large prize as the result of a random drawing subsequently concluded that he had in fact worked especially hard. This is an example of
    a. vivid, anecdotal information being more important than base-rate data
    b. disguised hostility
    c. outgroup bias
    d. belief in a just world

35. Forming a new stereotype of "serious, college-bound young people" to protect one's larger negative stereotype of irresponsible teenagers is an example of
    a. just world thinking
    b. authoritarianism
    c. subtyping
    d. external attribution

36. The most recent explanation which social psychologists have offered for prejudice emphasizes _____ sources.
    a. social
    b. cognitive
    c. emotional
    d. political

37. According to the text, stereotypes are resistant to change because
    a. for the most part, they are accurate reflections of reality
    b. our prejudgments influence how we interpret and process information
    c. they are always based in an authoritarian attitude which is blind to disconfirming evidence
    d. they are held by people with low intelligence

38. When Steve Spencer and his colleagues (1999) gave a very difficult math test to men and women students and said that women performed as well as men on the test, the women
    a. outperformed the men
    b. did in fact perform more poorly than the men
    c. performed as well as the men
    d. with more liberal attitudes outperformed the women with more conservative attitudes

39. Research by Faye Crosby and her colleagues (1989) has found that women
    a. believe that sex discrimination does not affect themselves but rather other working women
    b. report being personally discriminated against at work
    c. believe that sex discrimination affects most working women and report being personally discriminated against at work
    d. neither believe that sex discrimination affects most working women nor report being personally discriminated against at work

40. The "personal/group discrimination discrepancy" refers to the finding that
    a. individuals deny being personally discriminated against but see their groups as victims
    b. individuals believe they are personally discriminated against but not their groups
    c. many people show prejudice toward individuals but not toward their groups
    d. many people show prejudice toward groups but not toward their individual members

SHORT ESSAY QUESTIONS

Answer the following questions in the space provided.

1. Distinguish among prejudice, discrimination, and racism.

2. What evidence indicates that prejudice and stereotyping still exist in Canada?

3. Describe the evidence that subtle forms of prejudice exist and explain how this subtle prejudice may affect interpersonal interactions.

4. Explain how unequal status breeds prejudice.

5. Explain how identifying ourselves by group membership can contribute to ingroup bias.

6. Identify characteristics of the authoritarian personality.

7. Explain how our mood affects our feelings of prejudice.

8. Describe two ways in which our normal thinking processes may be a source of prejudice.

9. Describe how victims of prejudice, stereotyping and discrimination may reaction.

ANSWER KEY

Chapter Review

1. prejudgment
   stereotypes

2. behaviour
   sexism

3. prejudice
   multicultural
   subtle
   behaviour
   exaggerated

4. explicit
   implicit
   stereotype

5. Unequal
   conflict
   resources

6. ingroup
   groups
   favouritism
   prejudice

7. conformity

8. Ethnocentric
   authoritarian
   punitive

9. Frustration
   displaced
   low

10. negatively

ambivalent
benevolent
discrimination

11. prejudicial
    homogeneity
    group

12. Distinctive
    group
    illusory

13. Attribution
    group-serving
    just

14. interpretations
    perpetuating
    unknown
    extremely

15. control
    depressed
    esteem
    prejudice

16. self-fulfilling
    confirm
    stereotype

17. gender
    deny
    discrepancy
    control
    difficult

Matching Terms

1. e
2. l
3. i
4. m
5. j
6. c
7. h

8. f
9. n
10. d
11. k
12. g
13. b
14. a

True-False Review

1.	F		14.	F
2.	T		15.	F
3.	T		16.	F
4.	T		17.	T
5.	T		18.	T
6.	T		19.	F
7.	T		20.	T
8.	T		21.	T
9.	T		22.	F
10.	F		23.	F
11.	F		24.	F
12.	F		25.	T
13.	F			

Multiple-Choice Practice Test

1.	c		21.	a
2.	d		22.	d
3.	c		23.	c
4.	a		24.	a
5.	c		25.	a
6.	a		26.	a
7.	d		27.	b
8.	c		28.	a
9.	c		29.	c
10.	c		30.	b
11.	b		31.	a
12.	d		32.	d
13.	d		33.	b
14.	a		34.	d
15.	d		35.	c
16.	b		36.	b
17.	c		37.	b
18.	d		38.	b
19.	c		39.	a
20.	c		40.	a

CHAPTER 13
CONFLICT AND PEACEMAKING

CHAPTER OBJECTIVES

After completing your study of this chapter you should be able to:

1. Define conflict.
2. Explain how the pursuit of self-interest can produce a social dilemma.
3. Suggest specific ways of resolving social dilemmas.
4. Describe how competition produces conflict.
5. Describe how most people define justice.
6. Identify specific misperceptions that fuel conflict.
7. Describe the conditions under which close contact reduces hostility between opposing parties.
8. Explain how superordinate goals reduce conflict.
9. Discuss how bargaining, mediation, and arbitration can be used to resolve differences between opposing parties.
10. Describe the GRIT model for reducing conflict.

CHAPTER REVIEW

Supply the words necessary to complete each of the following statements.

CONFLICT

1. Conflict is a _____ incompatibility of actions or goals.

2. Social dilemmas such as nuclear arms, global warming, overpopulation, and natural resource depletion are the result of various parties rationally pursuing their _____ - _____ to their collective _____. The _____ Dilemma and the Tragedy of the _____ games have been used to study how well-meaning people easily become trapped in mutually destructive behaviour.

3. Research with laboratory dilemmas suggests that cooperation can be promoted by _____ behaviour for the common good, by keeping social groups _____ so that people feel responsibility for one another, by allowing people to _____ which reduces mistrust, by changing the payoffs to make _____ more rewarding, and by appealing to _____ norms.

4. _____ for scarce resources can also breed conflict. In a series of famous experiments, Sherif divided boys into two groups and found that win- _____ competition triggered outright warfare.

5. Many people believe the criterion for justice is _____, in which the distribution of rewards is in _____ to individuals' contributions. When people feel exploited, they may accept and _____ their inferior position, demand _____, or attempt to restore equity by _____.

6. Conflicts often contain only a small core of truly incompatible goals but are surrounded by many _____ of the other's motives and goals. Opposing parties often have _____-_____ perceptions: Each side attributes similar virtues to themselves and similar vices to the other side. Characteristically, such images are often self-_____. International conflicts are also fed by the illusion of an evil _____—good _____ perception. Conflict will continue until the parties work at _____ their differences.

PEACEMAKING

7. Numerous studies confirm that contact promotes _____ group interaction. Contacts that promote equal status and _____, a common group _____, and expose multiple group memberships while maintaining that members of the conflicting groups are typical members are more likely to reduce _____.

8. In his boys' camp experiments, Sherif demonstrated how conflict between groups promotes _____ within groups when facing a common external threat. He introduced _____ goals to reconcile opposing groups. Similarly this has been Canada's goal in championing the value of _____. Generalizing from positive interracial experiences may be enhanced by initially _____ group diversity, then acknowledging it, then _____ it.

9. When conflicts are not intense or at an impasse, opposing parties may _____ directly, that is, seek agreement through direct negotiation. Sometimes a third-party _____ can help antagonists by replacing their win-_____ view of the conflict with a more cooperative win-_____ orientation. Such a person can reduce self-fulfilling _____ and increase mutual understanding and _____ between opposing sides. _____ is resolution of a conflict by a neutral third party who studies both sides and imposes a solution.

10. Sometimes tension is so high that genuine communication becomes impossible. In such cases, small _____ acts by one party may elicit reciprocal actions from the other. In Osgood's _____ model, one party to a conflict _____ its conciliatory intent, invites the adversary to _____ carries out several verifiable conciliatory _____, but maintains its _____ capability.

MATCHING TERMS

Write the letter of the correct term from the right before the appropriate number on the left.

_____ 1. Uses conciliation to reduce tension.

_____ 2. Groups of boys involved in Sherif's experiments on how competition produces conflict.

_____ 3. A laboratory demonstration of the tragedy of the commons.

_____ 4. A third party imposes a settlement.

_____ 5. On any given trial in this game, one is better off confessing.

_____ 6. The distribution of rewards in proportion to individuals' contributions.

_____ 7. The result of creatively managed conflict.

_____ 8. Arab and Israeli views.

_____ 9. An approach that values and appreciates all cultures.

_____ 10. Contact between opposing groups must be of this sort if it is to reduce conflict.

_____ 11. A perceived incompatibility of goals.

_____ 12. The opposing parties seek agreement through direct negotiation.

_____ 13. A common shared goal that reduces conflict.

_____ 14. A third party facilitates communication between two opposing groups.

a. Edney's Nuts Game

b. equity

c. superordinate goal

d. mirror-image perceptions

e. Rattlers and Eagles

f. GRIT

g. multiculturalism

h. equal status

i. mediation

j. arbitration

k. bargaining

l. Prisoners' Dilemma

m. conflict

n. peace

TRUE-FALSE REVIEW

Circle T if the statement is true and F if it is false.

T F 1. Conflict is always a destructive drain on human potential.

T F 2. Encouraging people to pursue their individual self-interest is often an effective antidote to social dilemmas.

T F 3. The laboratory dilemmas provide examples of how well-meaning people become trapped into mutually destructive behaviour.

T F 4. In the Prisoners' Dilemma, a person always receives the best payoff on a particular trial if he or she cooperates.

T F 5. In laboratory games those who are 100 percent cooperative are rarely exploited.

T F 6. The "tragedy of the commons" refers to the loss of one's personal property when it is taken over by the government.

T F 7. The Prisoners' Dilemma is an example of a non-zero-sum game.

T F 8. Self-serving behaviour always results in collective doom.

T F 9. In laboratory dilemmas people who realize that their self-serving choices are mutually destructive stop making them.

T F 10. After reading about the commons dilemma, theater patrons littered less than those who had read about voting.

T F 11. Sherif's experiments in a boys' summer camp demonstrated how competition can produce social conflict.

T F 12. Equity involves the distribution of rewards in proportion to individuals' needs.

T F 13. All cultures tend to define justice in terms of equity.

T F 14. Conflicts often contain only a small number of truly incompatible goals.

T F 15. Studies of American and Soviet political statements indicated that while Americans preferred mutual disarmament, the Soviets preferred to obtain military superiority.

T F 16. People with opposing views on issues such as abortion and capital punishment often differ less than they suppose.

T F 17. Student exchange programs invariably improve students' attitudes toward their host countries.

T F 18. Forming a friendship with one outgroup member will have no effect on developing positive attitudes towards the whole outgroup.

T F 19. Sherif used arbitration to reduce conflict in the boys' summer camp.

T F 20. Canada's policy of multiculturalism is an example of using a superordinate goal to promote harmony among groups rather than conflict.

T F 21. Mediation involves resolution of a conflict by a third party who studies both sides and imposes a settlement.

T F 22. Integrative agreements are win-win agreements that reconcile both parties' interests to their mutual benefit.

T F 23. If you want to buy a new car at the best price, adopting a tough bargaining stance by opening with a very low offer generally backfires.

T F 24. GRIT uses conciliation to reduce conflict.

T F 25. Lester B. Pearson's handling of the Suez Canal Crisis in 1956 demonstrates how arbitration can reduce conflict.

MULTIPLE-CHOICE PRACTICE TEST

Circle the correct letter.

1. Which of the following is true of conflict?
    a. without conflict, people seldom face and resolve their problems.
    b. conflict always involves a real incompatibility of goals
    c. social psychologists have studied interpersonal but not international conflict
    d. social psychologists have not been able to study conflict in a laboratory setting

2. Two gas station owners in Roseville cut their gas prices in order to capture a portion of their competitor's business. However, neither gained any of the other's customers and in the long run both operated at a loss. This outcome best illustrates the dynamics of
    a. a social dilemma
    b. the GRIT strategy
    c. an inequitable relationship
    d. mirror-image perceptions

3. In playing the laboratory version of Prisoners' Dilemma, a person's outcome from <u>any given decision</u> will be better if he or she
    a. cooperates
    b. defects
    c. cooperates only if the other person cooperates
    d. cooperates only if the other person defects

4. Edney's Nuts Game
    a. is a non-zero-sum game played between two persons
    b. demonstrates how mirror-image perceptions can increase conflict
    c. demonstrates how conciliation reduces conflict
    d. illustrates the tragedy of the commons

5. In non-zero-sum games,
    a. one player always wins and the other always loses
    b. one player's winnings equal the other player's losses
    c. both players may win, both may lose, or one may win and the other may lose
    d. the players' combined outcomes can never equal zero

6. When Kaori Sato used a simulated forest to study the Commons Dilemma in a communal culture, he found
   a. results much like those obtained in western cultures
   b. that people were much more cooperative than in western cultures
   c. females but not males were more cooperative than their counterparts in western cultures
   d. adults but not children were more cooperative than their counterparts in western cultures

7. The tragedy of the commons illustrates how
   a. communism leads to economic ruin
   b. self-serving behaviour leads to collective doom
   c. false stereotypes lead to social conflict
   d. superordinate goals may fail to produce cooperation in capitalistic societies

8. The _____ the commons, the _____ responsibility each person feels for it.
   a. smaller; more
   b. larger; more
   c. more important; more
   d. more important; less

9. Research on laboratory dilemmas reveals that cooperation is facilitated if
   a. one person is 100 percent cooperative
   b. the opponents can communicate with one another
   c. the game is changed into a zero-sum game
   d. the size of the payoffs is increased

10. When Robyn Dawes and his colleagues gave people a short sermon about group benefits, exploitation, and ethics before they played a dilemma game,
    a. people reacted by playing even more competitively
    b. people were more cooperative in their play
    c. people ignored the sermon and their play was unchanged
    d. females were more cooperative and males were more competitive

11. Social dilemmas can be resolved by all of the following except
    a. legislating laws
    b. keeping the group large so all interested parties can be included
    c. making exploitation less rewarding
    d. encouraging social responsibility

12. Appeals to altruistic norms
    a. have proven to be helpful in reducing social dilemmas
    b. work in resolving small-scale but not large-scale dilemmas
    c. create reactance and make people more competitive
    d. worked to resolve conflict in the Nuts Game but not in the Prisoners' Dilemma

13. Sherif's studies of conflict in summer camp should lead one to suggest which of the following to a couple having marital difficulties?
    a. play poker, keeping a cumulative score
    b. encounter each other: express your true feelings
    c. work together on something
    d. take separate vacations

14. Rodney and Ralph are twin brothers who each contributed $75 to purchase a new bicycle. Rodney rides it 75 percent of the time. This would be an example of
    a. an inequitable relationship
    b. the tragedy of the commons
    c. a zero-sum relationship
    d. mirror-image perceptions

15. In Japan, pay is more often based on _____ and less often based on

    _____ .
    a. need; equality
    b. education; experience
    c. seniority; productivity
    d. potential; achievement

16. When Gregory Mitchell and his colleagues asked American University students what standard of justice they would prefer if their own place on the economic ladder was unknown, they indicated that they would prefer
    a. that resources be distributed equally
    b. that resources be distributed on the basis of productivity
    c. enough priority placed on equality to meet their own needs but also some reward for productivity
    d. that goods be distributed strictly on the basis of need

17. The tendency of each party to a conflict to see itself as moral and peaceloving and the other as evil and aggressive is known as
    a. reciprocal illusory perceptions
    b. the fundamental attribution error
    c. illusory correlation
    d. mirror-image perception

18. John believes he is hard-working but his wife Rachel is lazy. Rachel believes she is hard-working but John is lazy. This is an example of
    a. an inequitable relationship
    b. mirror-image perception
    c. a superordinate conflict
    d. a social trap

19. According to a review of studies that have investigated the contact hypothesis conducted by Pettigrew and his colleagues (1999), what effect does contact between members of opposing groups have on intergroup relations?
    a. contact promotes harmony between groups
    b. contact promotes animosity between groups
    c. contact has little effect on intergroup relations
    d. contact occasionally promotes harmony between groups but usually promotes animosity

20. Contact between opposing racial groups reduces hostility
    a. if it occurs in a competitive situation where parties are likely to communicate with each other
    b. if the minority group is given superior status
    c. if it is structured to convey equal status
    d. between younger members of the respective groups but not between older members

21. Canadians around the country cheered as the Toronto Maple Leafs hockey team beat the Detroit Red Wings and won the Stanley Cup. Social psychologists would say that the reason so many Canadians feel such a sense of national pride about this event is because
    a. Canadians like to beat Americans in sports
    b. hockey promotes a positive attitude of nationalism
    c. winning the game is a superordinate goal
    d. a common external threat unifies groups

22. Sherif's experiments in a boys' summer camp demonstrated how _____
    reduce conflict.
    a. appeals to altruistic norms
    b. regulations
    c. communications
    d. superordinate goals

23. Shared goals that necessitate cooperative effort are said to be
    a. reciprocal
    b. superordinate
    c. equitable
    d. companionate

24. Conflict between groups promotes _____ within groups.
    a. unity
    b. conflict
    c. concern for equity
    d. role confusion

25. Which of the following best illustrates a superordinate goal?
    a. a student who has been failing psychology works hard to get "As" in her other classes
    b. a woman listens to her friend's problems even though she finds them boring
    c. local people work together to clean up a neighbourhood park
    d. a husband and wife work together cleaning the garage

26. A cooperative effort engaged in by two previously conflicting groups
    a. always has the long-term effect of boosting the groups' attraction to one another
    b. may actually increase tension between the two groups if the effort is unsuccessful
    c. will only be effective in reducing long-term tensions if engaging in the effort was
       suggested by a mediator
    d. typically reduces long-term conflict between opposing groups of males but not
       between opposing groups of females

27. We are most likely to generalize positive interracial experiences with a few individuals to a
    more positive attitude toward a whole outgroup if we perceive
    a. the outgroup as being as diverse as our own group
    b. the individuals as being representative of their group rather than as atypical
    c. ourselves as the only members from our own group having positive experiences with
       the outgroup
    d. the individuals as high in social status within the outgroup

28. People are likely to have high self-esteem if they have a _____ ethnic identity and a _____ mainstream cultural identity.
    a. weak; weak
    b. weak; strong
    c. strong; weak
    d. strong; strong

29. Milton, a Jewish-American, lacks a real sense of either his Jewish or his American identity. Milton is especially likely to experience
    a. mirror-image perceptions
    b. ingroup bias
    c. low self-esteem
    d. the tragedy of the commons

30. A couple who decide to divorce agree to meet with a third party to work out a joint custody arrangement. This is an example of
    a. the GRIT approach
    b. bargaining
    c. mediation
    d. negotiation

31. Bargaining tough is likely to backfire
    a. when the conflict is over a pie of fixed size
    b. when the conflict is over a pie that can shrink
    c. when females bargain tough with males
    d. in virtually every situation

32. Compared to compromises, integrative agreements are
    a. more enduring and lead to better ongoing relationships
    b. only reached through mediation or arbitration
    c. only possible when perceived injustice is the cause of conflict
    d. less likely to lead to a permanent settlement

33. Kevin and Joel, two teenage brothers, are fighting over the evening newspaper. Knowing Kevin only wants the sports section and Joel only wants the latest stock quotations, their mother takes the paper and gives each boy the section containing the news of interest. In this case the mother arrived at a(n)
    a. mutual compromise
    b. cooperative settlement
    c. enlightened consensus
    d. integrative agreement

34. A key factor in determining whether people will communicate constructively and thereby correct misperceptions is
    a. their trust that the opposing side is well-intentioned
    b. their verbal fluency
    c. if each party sticks to statements of fact and refrains from stating how they feel about the other's actions
    d. if information which contradicts the other party's misperceptions is given bit by bit and not all at once

35. The GRIT strategy was formulated as a plan
    a. for reversing conflict through conciliation
    b. for decreasing interracial tensions in desegregated schools
    c. to demonstrate how conflict in general can be reduced through arbitration
    d. to demonstrate how regulation can alleviate social dilemmas

36. In the "final-offer arbitration," the third party settles a conflict by
    a. choosing between the final offers made by each side
    b. compromising between the final offers made by each side
    c. providing an integrative agreement based on final offers from each side
    d. introducing a superordinate goal

37. Factory workers want a pay rate of $15 per hour and management offers $12 per hour. After weeks of conflict they agree to have a third party set the pay scale. After hearing both sides the third party sets the rate at $14. This is an example of resolving conflict through
    a. bargaining
    b. arbitration
    c. mediation
    d. conciliation

38. The GRIT model could be applied to the reduction of conflict between
    a. individuals
    b. groups
    c. nations
    d. all of these

39. Lester B. Pearson's interventions in the Suez Canal crisis were most similar to which of the following approaches to reducing conflict?
    a. equal status contact
    b. bargaining
    c. arbitration
    d. the GRIT model

40. According to the text, contact between two conflicting groups can often improve relationships and correct misperceptions. Which kind of contact is, however, least likely to have that effect?
    a. having the two groups participate on the same sports team
    b. having the two groups work together in the same factory
    c. placing one group in charge of the other group when carrying out work assignments
    d. having the two groups in the same classroom

SHORT ESSAY QUESTIONS

Answer the following questions in the space provided.

1. Define a social dilemma using examples.

2. Describe the "tragedy of the commons" and explain its causes.

3. List three possible ways of promoting cooperation in the Prisoners' Dilemma game.

4. Briefly describe how Sherif first increased and then decreased conflict in a boys' summer camp.

5. Give the formula for an equitable relationship.

6. Describe two factors that make it more likely that intergroup contact will improve intergroup relations.

7. Distinguish among bargaining, mediation, and arbitration.

8. Describe the GRIT strategy for reducing conflict.

ANSWER KEY

Chapter Review

1. perceived

2. self-interest
   detriment
   Prisoners'
   Commons

3. regulating
   small
   communicate
   cooperation
   altruistic

4. Competition
   lose

5. equity
   proportion
   justify
   compensation
   retaliating

6. misperceptions
   mirror-image
   confirming
   leader
   people
   reconciling

7. positive
   friendships
   identity
   conflict

8. unity
   superordinate
   multiculturalism
   minimizing
   transcending

9. bargain
   mediator
   lose
   win
   misperceptions
   trust
   Arbitration

10. conciliatory
    GRIT
    announces
    reciprocate
    acts
    retaliatory

Matching Terms

1. f
2. e
3. a
4. j
5. l
6. b
7. n

8. d
9. g
10. h
11. m
12. k
13. c
14. i

True-False Review

1.	F	14.	T
2.	F	15.	T
3.	T	16.	T
4.	F	17.	F
5.	F	18.	F
6.	F	19.	F
7.	T	20.	T
8.	F	21.	F
9.	F	22.	T
10.	T	23.	F
11.	T	24.	T
12.	F	25.	F
13.	F		

Multiple-Choice Practice Test

1.	a	21.	d
2.	a	22.	d
3.	b	23.	b
4.	d	24.	a
5.	c	25.	c
6.	a	26.	b
7.	b	27.	b
8.	a	28.	d
9.	b	29.	c
10.	b	30.	c
11.	b	31.	b
12.	a	32.	a
13.	c	33.	d
14.	a	34.	a
15.	c	35.	a
16.	c	36.	a
17.	d	37.	b
18.	b	38.	d
19.	a	39.	d
20.	c	40.	c

MODULE A
SOCIAL PSYCHOLOGY IN THE CLINIC

CHAPTER OBJECTIVES

After completing your study of this chapter you should be able to:

1. Describe how thinking errors may contaminate the personality interpretations made by mental health professionals.
2. Discuss implications of illusory thinking principles for psychology as a scientific discipline.
3. Describe the thought patterns of depressed persons and discuss whether their attributions are a cause or consequence of their depressed mood.
4. Describe the thought patterns associated with loneliness and social anxiety.
5. Discuss factors influencing people's reactions to illness and the role of negative emotions in health.
6. Discuss the links between close, supportive relationships and well-being.

CHAPTER REVIEW

Supply the words necessary to complete each of the following statements.

1. Social psychology seeks answers to: how to improve our _____ and predictions about others; how do the ways we _____about ourselves and others feed our problems; how can we reverse _____thought patterns; what part do close, supportive _____play in our health and happiness.

MAKING CLINICAL JUDGMENTS

2. Professional clinical judgments are also social judgments, and thus subject to its principles. _____ _____ is evident when clinicians perceive expected relationships between test performances and symptoms when no relationship exists. After-the-fact psychologizing is particularly vulnerable to the _____ bias.

3. When interacting with clients, erroneous diagnoses are often _____-_____ since interviewers tend to seek out and recall information which _____ whatever they are looking for. The behaviours of people undergoing psychotherapy may come to fit the _____ of their therapists. As a result, most clinicians express more _____in their _____assessments than in _____ data. Although statistical predictions may be unreliable, human _____ is even more unreliable.

4. Research on _____ thinking points to a need to test
_____ before presenting them as truth. The goal of every
_____ is to seek hard facts.

SOCIAL COGNITION IN PROBLEM BEHAVIOURS

5. Although depressed people are _____ thinkers, research indicates that they
make surprisingly _____ judgments. Depressed people are more likely to
attribute failure to causes that are _____, global, and
_____.

6. Our _____ color our thinking. Depression definitely has both cognitive and
_____ consequences. At the same time, evidence suggests that a
pessimistic _____ style contributes to depressive reactions.

7. Those who suffer chronic _____ and states of social _____ are
also caught in a vicious cycle of self-defeating social _____ and social
_____. _____ is a form of social anxiety characterized by
self-consciousness and worry about what others think.

8. The new subfield of _____ psychology provides psychology's
contribution to _____ medicine. It explores how people decide they are
_____, how they explain their _____, and when they seek and
follow _____. Heart disease has been linked with an _____-
_____ personality. Research suggests that an attitude of
_____ is good for health.

SOCIAL SUPPORT AND WELL-BEING

9. Close, supportive relationships promote _____ and happiness. Such
relationships help us cope with _____ events, especially when they
enable people to _____ their painful feels. Feelings of
_____ and support, together with health care and nutrition factors, help
explain why _____ status corresponds with _____.

10. Close relationships also foster _____. Throughout the world,
_____ people report greater happiness and are less at risk for
_____.

MATCHING TERMS

Write the letter of the correct term from the right before the appropriate number on the left.

_____ 1. About 10 percent of men and 20 percent of women will experience it.

_____ 2. A distinguishing feature of depressed persons.

_____ 3. Psychology's contribution to behavioural medicine.

_____ 4. May serve a self-handicapping function.

_____ 5. More common among adolescents than among adults.

_____ 6. Occurs when we are uncertain about our ability to impress others.

_____ 7. Integrates behavioural and medical knowledge about disease.

_____ 8. Good for health.

_____ 9. Patients come to fit the theories of their therapists.

_____ 10. Linked with heart disease.

_____ 11. One's habitual way of explaining life's events.

_____ 12. The study, assessment, and treatment of people with psychological difficulties.

a. clinical psychology

b. loneliness

c. major depressive episode

d. explanatory style

e. health psychology

f. alcohol abuse

g. behavioural medicine

h. sadder-but-wiser

i. self-confirming diagnosis

j. anger-prone personality

k. optimism

l. social anxiety

TRUE-FALSE REVIEW

Circle T if the statement is true and F if it is false.

T F 1. In the hands of an experienced clinician, the Draw-a-Person test has very high predictive validity.

T F 2. Because of the ambiguity of their work, clinical psychologists tend to lack confidence in the accuracy of their judgments.

T F 3. In analyzing the childhood experiences of their clients, therapists can easily give after-the-fact interpretations that confirm their theories.

T F 4. After David Rosenhan alerted mental hospital staff members that pseudopatients might seek admission to their hospital, staff were much more accurate in recognizing real patients and those persons who were normal.

T F 5. Intuitive or clinical predictions tend to be more reliable than statistical predictions.

T F 6. The best predictor of success in graduate school is provided by the assessment of a trained interviewer.

T F 7. Research has indicated that depressed persons may be more accurate than nondepressives in estimating their degree of control over the environment.

T F 8. Depressed people are more likely than nondepressed people to blame themselves for their own failures.

T F 9. Depression is both a cause and a consequence of negative cognitions.

T F 10. In North America, young adults today are three times as likely as their grandparents to have suffered depression.

T F 11. Males and females feel lonely under somewhat different conditions.

T F 12. Lonely people seem to have more negative perceptions of others.

T F 13. Lonely people are more likely to talk about themselves and show little interest in their conversational partner.

T F   14. Anxious people are more likely to feel less anxious if they drink alcohol alone in a quiet room.

T F   15. Students studying psychology are prone to attribute their psychological symptoms to newly learned disorders.

T F   16. Women's physical and mental skills fluctuate noticeably with their menstrual cycles.

T F   17. Social psychology has contributed to the understanding but not to the treatment of psychological disorders.

T F   18. Mildly depressed people are more vulnerable to heart disease.

T F   19. Optimists recover faster from surgery than pessimists.

T F   20. Close relationships promote psychological but not physical health.

T F   21. Confiding in friends makes you feel worse because you relive the pain every time you tell your story.

T F   22. Collectivists generally report greater life satisfaction than individualists.

T F   23. The happiest university students are those who feel satisfied with their love life.

T F   24. Three out of four married people say their spouse is their best friend.

T F   25. Rates of suicide and depression are higher among the nonmarried.

MULTIPLE-CHOICE PRACTICE TEST

Circle the correct letter.

1. According to the text, social psychology has contributed to all of the following <u>except</u>
   a. our understanding of psychological disorders
   b. why people seek treatment of psychological disorders
   c. improving the process of clinical judgment and prediction
   d. the definition of psychological disorder

2. The text suggests that clinicians may continue to have confidence in uninformative or ambiguous tests because of human susceptibility to
   a. the inoculation effect
   b. learned helplessness
   c. the representativeness heuristic
   d. illusory correlation

3. After complaining of hearing voices, David Rosenhan and his associates were diagnosed as schizophrenic and hospitalized. Clinicians' subsequent attempts to explain the diagnosis demonstrated
   a. the bias in after-the-fact explanations
   b. the fundamental attribution error
   c. their susceptibility to the just world phenomenon
   d. the benefits of clinical intuition

4. What error in thinking may contribute to a person's feeling of guilt after a close relative commits suicide?
   a. self-serving bias
   b. the fundamental attribution error
   c. hindsight bias
   d. depressive realism

5. From the material presented in the text, which of the following is an accurate statement?
   a. clinical psychologists are more susceptible to illusory thinking than are social psychologists
   b. projective tests actually give more useful information than do objective tests
   c. people who come for therapy want to hear negative things about themselves
   d. behaviours of people undergoing psychotherapy come to fit the theories of their therapists

6. Gayle, a Freudian analyst, finds that, without exception, her patients report dreams closely related to their emotional problems and are easily understood in terms of Freud's theory of personality. From research presented in the text, what may best explain why the dreams and problems of Gayle's patients are so consistent with Freudian theory?
   a. Freud's theory is the oldest and most comprehensive of all the theories of personality
   b. Freud's theory is more ambiguous than any other theory, and thus any problem fits into its framework
   c. the patients are perhaps induced to give information that is consistent with Gayle's theoretical orientation
   d. Freudian psychotherapists are "true believers" and Gayle's report is an attempt to convert other therapists to her orientation

7. The results from research conducted by the Ministry of the Solicitor General found that the best predictor of future offending by mentally disordered criminals was
   a. the clinical prediction
   b. the past history of criminal behaviour
   c. the offender's personal prediction
   d. the prediction of correctional officers

8. Robyn Dawes, writing In House of Cards: Psychology and Psychotherapy Built on Myth, reports that interviewers' ratings of medical school applicants were highly predictive of the applicants'
   a. likelihood of receiving the M.D.
   b. eventual performance in their first year of residency
   c. likelihood of graduating from medical school with honors
   d. none of the above

9. Research evidence suggests that mental health workers
   a. are relatively immune to the illusion of control
   b. should rely more heavily on clinical intuition than on statistical prediction
   c. are too readily convinced of their own after-the-fact analyses
   d. are more susceptible to illusory thinking than are social psychologists

10. According to the text, the pervasiveness of illusory thinking points to the need for a _____ study of thought and behaviour.
   a. psychohistorical
   b. scientific
   c. literary
   d. humanistic

11. Studies of depression challenge the common presumption that
    a. depressed people are negative thinkers
    b. more women than men suffer major depressive episodes
    c. depressed people are unrealistic
    d. a depressed mood has both cognitive and behavioural consequences

12. Which of the following attributions regarding a failure or setback illustrates the <u>stable</u> quality of a depressed person's explanatory style?
    a. "It's all my fault."
    b. "It's going to last forever."
    c. "The whole world is against me."
    d. "It's going to affect everything I do."

13. When researchers had relatively depressed and nondepressed college students observe whether their pressing a button was linked with whether a light came on, the results indicated that the
    a. depressed underestimated their degree of control
    b. depressed were quite accurate in estimating their degree of control
    c. nondepressed were quite accurate in estimating their degree of control
    d. nondepressed underestimated their degree of control

14. Compared to nondepressed people, depressed people are more likely to attribute their failures and setbacks to causes that are
    a. unstable
    b. internal
    c. specific
    d. situational

15. Philip suffers from chronic depression. How is he likely to respond when told that he failed the test to renew his driver's license?
    a. "Yesterday was just my unlucky day."
    b. "I imagine very few people have passed that same test."
    c. "The person giving the test is incompetent."
    d. "I am a poor driver and always will be."

16. Valerie is a mildly depressed college student. From research presented in the text on depression she
    a. probably suffers from the better-than-average phenomenon
    b. assumes that her behaviour is well-accepted by others
    c. demonstrates the sadder-but-wiser effect
    d. is below average in intelligence

233

17. Research on the social thinking of those vulnerable to depression indicates that
    a. depression is both a cause and a consequence of their negative thinking
    b. they have surprisingly positive self-concepts
    c. males and females who are depressed think very differently
    d. they are more vulnerable to both illusory correlation and the fundamental attribution error

18. According to Martin Seligman, the decline of religion and family and the growth of the "you can do it" idea have contributed to a large increase in
    a. character disorders
    b. phobias
    c. schizophrenia
    d. depression

19. Research on loneliness indicates that
    a. females are more likely to experience loneliness than males
    b. lonely people are more realistic than those who do not report feelings of loneliness
    c. loneliness coincides with aloneness
    d. lonely people tend to perceive others in negative ways

20. Chronically lonely people tend to blame _____ for their poor social relationships.
    a. their parents or early childhood experiences
    b. themselves
    c. the uncaring attitudes of the people around them
    d. cultural values and patterns

21. In contrast to those who are not lonely, lonely people tend to
    a. spend more time talking about themselves when conversing with a stranger
    b. be more inclined to blame others for their problems
    c. be more susceptible to the illusion of control
    d. be more inclined to idealize members of the opposite sex

22. Which of the following situations would cause the greatest anxiety?
    a. your study group is discussing psychology, a course you really enjoy
    b. you are on a first date with a classmate
    c. you are going out to dinner with your best friend
    d. you are being interviewed for an important job

23. Bob goes to the local pub and drinks quite a few beers. While leaving the restroom, he sees a sign that says, "Don't drink and drive." Bob is probably
    a. less likely to drive home than his friend who has only had one beer
    b. more likely to drive home than his friend who has only had one beer
    c. no more or less likely to drive home than his friend who has only had one beer
    d. unaffected by seeing the sign

24. Dr. Jones is a psychologist who specializes in the causes and control of stress. Dr. Jones is most likely a(n) _____ psychologist.
    a. consumer
    b. forensic
    c. educational
    d. health

25. Studies on people's reactions to their own physical condition indicate that
    a. half or more of all heart attack victims die before seeking or receiving medical help
    b. college students tend to overreport medical complaints
    c. women's mental skills fluctuate noticeably with their menstrual cycle
    d. most people are good at estimating their blood pressure

26. Studies of women's fluctuations in mood around their menstrual periods reveal that
    a. most women experience mood fluctuations prior to their menstrual period
    b. a subset of women, but not most women, experience mood fluctuations prior to their menstrual period
    c. many women experience mood fluctuations during their menstrual period, but few women experience such mood fluctuation before their period
    d. there is little evidence that women's moods fluctuate across the menstrual cycle

27. During a musical performance, students began complaining to one another of headaches, nausea, and dizziness. Eventually, more than 200 became ill. Later investigations found no diagnosable illness nor environmental problem. This epidemic best illustrates the impact of
    a. perceived control on reactions to stress
    b. conditioning on the suppression of the immune system
    c. social influence on the interpretation of symptoms
    d. pessimism on physical health

28. Research has shown that women _____ than men.
    a. have higher rates of cancer
    b. use fewer prescription drugs
    c. visit physicians more frequently
    d. report fewer symptoms of illness

29. Research indicates that heart disease is most clearly linked with an _____ personality.
    a. introverted
    b. anger-prone
    c. apathetic
    d. assertive

30. Bill has been diagnosed with lung cancer. He is least likely to have the recommended operation if
    a. he has a good relationship with his doctor
    b. the doctor says the operation gives a 40% chance of survival
    c. the doctor says the operation gives a 60% chance of dying
    d. Bill and his doctor discuss the various options together

31. Members of baseball's Hall of Fame who offered pessimistic explanations for bad events such as losing big games
    a. died at younger ages
    b. were more susceptible to loneliness
    c. were less successful in life after retiring from baseball
    d. were more likely to be divorced

32. Rats injected with live cancer cells were more likely to die of tumors if they also received _____.
    a. escapable shock
    b. a high-fat diet
    c. inescapable shock
    d. moderate doses of radiation

33. Mary wants advice on how to cope with the stress of a new job. She would be best advised to approach her new job with a sense of
    a. skepticism and humility
    b. ambition and competitiveness
    c. urgency and time-consciousness
    d. control and optimism

34. Research suggests that an attitude of _____ is generally good for health.
    a. competitiveness
    b. skepticism
    c. optimism
    d. humility

35. Research suggests that optimists
    a. recover more slowly from coronary bypass surgery
    b. tend to offer stable, global, and internal explanations for bad events
    c. may see themselves as invulnerable and thus fail to take sensible precautions
    d. are less susceptible to depression but more susceptible to anxiety

36. Compared with college women who have experienced nonsexual traumas, sexually abused women reported more health problems especially if
    a. they had kept their secret to themselves
    b. the abuser was a relative
    c. they were high in self-monitoring
    d. they were planning to marry in the next year

37. When people are asked, "What is necessary for your happiness?" most mention _____ first.
    a. meaningful work
    b. close personal relationships
    c. money
    d. good physical and mental health

38. In studies in a number of countries, researchers have found that
    a. being married is unrelated to happiness
    b. married people report being happier than unmarried people
    c. being married is associated with happiness for men but not for women
    d. being married is associated with happiness for women but not for men

39. Research on the relationship between marriage and happiness indicates that
    a. married men but not married women are happier than their single counterparts
    b. people who say their marriage is satisfying rarely report being unhappy or depressed
    c. about one-third of married Canadians say their marriage is "very happy"
    d. happiness seems to promote marriage but marriage does not promote happiness

40. Satisfaction with _____ seems to be the best predictor of overall happiness.
    a. work
    b. finances
    c. marriage
    d. community

SHORT ESSAY QUESTIONS

Answer the following questions in the space provided.

1. Explain how each of the following may characterize the judgments of mental health professionals:

    A. Illusory correlation

    B. Hindsight bias

    C. Self-fulfilling prophecy

2. Describe the thought patterns of depressed people. Is their attributional style the cause or the consequence of their depressed mood?

3. Describe the thought patterns associated with loneliness and social anxiety.

4. Explain how people's reactions to experiencing symptoms can affect their health?

5. Contrast how optimistic and pessimistic thinking can affect illness and health.

6. Briefly describe how social relations may influence health and happiness.

ANSWER KEY

Chapter Review

1. judgments
   think
   maladaptive
   relationships

2. Illusory
   correlation
   hindsight

3. self-confirming
   confirms
   theories
   confidence
   intuitive
   statistical
   intuition

4. illusory
   preconceptions
   science

5. negative
   accurate
   stable
   internal

6. moods

   behavioural
   explanatory

7. loneliness
   anxiety
   cognitions
   behaviours
   Shyness

8. health
   behavioural
   ill
   symptoms
   treatment
   anger-prone
   optimism

9. health
   stressful
   confide
   control
   economic
   longevity

10. happiness
    married
    depression

Matching Terms

1. c
2. h
3. e
4. f
5. b
6. l

7. g
8. k
9. i
10. j
11. d
12. a

True-False Review

1. F
2. F
3. T
4. F
5. F
6. F
7. T
8. T
9. T
10. T
11. T
12. T
13. T

14. F
15. T
16. F
17. F
18. T
19. T
20. F
21. F
22. T
23. T
24. T
25. T

Multiple-Choice Practice Test

1. d		21. a	
2. d		22. d	
3. a		23. a	
4. c		24. d	
5. d		25. a	
6. c		26. d	
7. b		27. c	
8. d		28. c	
9. c		29. b	
10. b		30. c	
11. c		31. a	
12. b		32. c	
13. b		33. d	
14. b		34. c	
15. d		35. c	
16. c		36. a	
17. a		37. b	
18. d		38. b	
19. d		39. b	
20. b		40. c	

MODULE B
SOCIAL PSYCHOLOGY IN COURT

CHAPTER OBJECTIVES

After completing your study of this chapter you should be able to:
1. Identify social psychology issues pertinent to the legal system.
2. Discuss findings on eyewitness testimony and describe ways of reducing error.
3. Identify defendant characteristics that may influence jurors' judgments and describe the effects of the judge's instructions on a jury.
4. Explain what can influence how jurors form judgements.
5. Discuss group influences that impact a jury.
6. Explain the value of simulated juries.

CHAPTER REVIEW

Supply the words necessary to complete each of the following statements.
1. We can think of the courtroom as a miniature social world; here, as elsewhere, people think about and _____ one another.

EYEWITNESS TESTIMONY
2. Experiments suggest that jurors find eyewitnesses _____, sometimes even those whose testimony is _____. In general, eyewitnesses' certainty about their judgments relates only modestly to their _____.

3. Errors creep in because we construct our _____ based partly on what we perceived at the time and partly on our expectations, beliefs, and current knowledge. _____ what happened commits people to their recollections, whether accurate or not. In addition, people tend to adjust what they say to _____ their listeners and then come to _____ the altered message. Receiving confirming _____ increases eyewitnesses' confidence in their judgments.

4. To increase the accuracy of eyewitnesses and jurors, experts suggest that we _____ police interviewers, minimize _____ lineup identifications, and educate jurors about _____ testimony.

OTHER INFLUENCES ON JUDGMENTS

5. The evidence usually is clear enough that jurors can set aside their _____
   and focus on the facts. But when the evidence is ambiguous, jurors may feel sympathetic to
   a defendant who is _____ or who is _____ to
   themselves. When the _____ is clear, jurors will focus their attention
   on it and their biases have minimal effect.

6. Jurors have difficulty following the judge's instructions to ignore
   _____ evidence. In fact, one experiment found that a judge's order to
   disregard testimony even _____ to the testimony's impact. This is
   especially so with _____ information that is vivid.

THE JURORS AS INDIVIDUALS AND GROUPS

7. In making decisions, jurors construct a story that makes sense of all
   the_____, consider the judge's _____, and
   compare their understanding with the possible _____.

8. Jurors may also have difficulty comprehending _____ and scientific
   information. Better decisions could be made if jurors had access to transcripts rather than
   relying on their _____ and if information was presented in
   _____, more effective ways using _____ language.

9. The chances are about 2 in _____ that jurors will initially not agree on a verdict.
   Yet after discussion, _____ percent emerge with a consensus.

10. The jury's verdict is usually the alternative favored by at least _____
    of the jurors at the outset. Without such a majority, a _____ jury is likely to
    result.

11. Jurors in the minority are likely to be most persuasive when they
    are_____, persistent, and self-confident, especially if they begin to
    trigger _____ from the majority. _____ jurors who have
    _____ social status tend to be most influential.

12. The finding that group deliberation leads high authoritarians to recommend
    _____ punishment and low authoritarians to recommend more
    _____ punishment suggest that group _____ can
    occur in juries. Through deliberations, initial leanings grow _____.

13. When evidence is not highly incriminating, juries tend to become _____ lenient
    after deliberating. A minority that favors acquittal has a _____
    chance of prevailing than one that favors conviction. To the extent that
    _____ influence moves jurors, we can hope that a jury's collective
    judgment will be superior to that of its average member.

FROM LAB TO LIFE: SIMULATED AND REAL JURIES

14. _____ juries are not real juries. However, the laboratory provides a practical method for studying important issues under _____ conditions. The jury experiment can mirror the complex world of the real _____ .

MATCHING TERMS

Write the letter of the correct term from the right before the appropriate number on the left.

_____ 1. Low authoritarians become more lenient, high authoritarians become more punitive.

_____ 2. The Crown Attorney during the trial, tries to enter evidence of a defendant's prior convictions.

_____ 3. Help researchers to formulate theories that can be used to interpret the complex world.

_____ 4. Persuasive but not always accurate.

_____ 5. May elicit reactance.

_____ 6. Technique to increase the amount and accuracy of recall.

_____ 7. Persuasive arguments.

_____ 8. Without it a hung jury is likely.

_____ 9. Benefits the defendant.

_____ 10. Jurors' personal biases are more likely to influence the verdict.

_____ 11. Favouring acquittal, it stands a better chance.

_____ 12. Remembering wrong information.

a. misinformation effect

b. physical attractiveness

c. information influence

d. judge's instructions

e. ambiguous cases

f. simulated juries

g. two-thirds majority

h. minority influence

i. group polarization

j. cognitive interview

k. inadmissible evidence

l. eyewitness testimony

TRUE-FALSE REVIEW

Circle T if the statement is true and F if it is false.

T F   1.   David Milgaard was convicted of murder based on inaccurate eyewitness testimony.

T F   2.   According to the text, social psychologists have conducted experiments on the courtroom because it provides an excellent context for studying the effect of the physical environment on behaviour.

T F   3.   Eyewitnesses who are shown to have poor eyesight may still have an impact on jurors' judgments.

T F   4.   An accurate eyewitness has a good memory for trivial details.

T F   5.   Eyewitnesses who are certain about their own testimony are more likely to be accurate.

T F   6.   Some judges have declared that one factor to be considered in judging eyewitness accuracy is the level of certainty demonstrated by the witness.

T F   7.   After suggestive questioning, witnesses may believe that a red light is actually green.

T F   8.   The more we retell a story, the more we may convince ourselves of a falsehood.

T F   9.   False memories feel and look like real memories.

T F   10.   A witness who dislikes the Crown Attorney is more likely to give testimony favourable to the defendant.

T F   11.   To increase eyewitness accuracy, interviewers should begin by allowing eyewitnesses to offer their own unprompted recollections.

T F   12.   Police line-ups always include a suspect.

T F   13.   False lineup identifications are reduced when witnesses simply make yes/no judgments in response to a sequence of people.

T F   14.   How a question is worded has little impact on what is remembered.

T F 15. Telling jurors that eyewitnesses are often inaccurate will have no impact on the weight given the testimony.

T F 16. Attractive defendants are treated more severely than unattractive defendants.

T F 17. A person accused of a politically motivated burglary is judged less guilty if his political views are similar to those of the jurors.

T F 18. When the evidence is clear and jurors focus on it, their biases seem to have minimal effect on their judgments.

T F 19. Jurors find it quite easy to disregard a rape victim's prior sexual history.

T F 20. Juries are more persuaded by evidence when it is presented in the order of a narrative story.

T F 21. Hung juries occur in about 20 percent of all jury trials.

T F 22. Most juries reach a verdict that was generally favoured at the beginning of deliberations.

T F 23. When the evidence is not highly incriminating, jurors tend to become more lenient after deliberating.

T F 24. A juror who favours a guilty verdict has more influence than one who favours acquittal.

T F 25. Simulated juries cannot provide helpful insights into the dynamics of actual courtrooms.

MULTIPLE-CHOICE PRACTICE TEST

Circle the correct letter.

1. In the case of David Milgaard, what had the greatest influence on his conviction for a murder that he did not commit?
   a. Milgaard's personal characteristics in the courtroom
   b. a minority influence by jurors
   c. eyewitness testimony
   d. scientific evidence

2. From the text, which of the following is a true statement regarding social psychology and the courtroom?
   a. most of the government research funds available to social psychologists have been designated for the study of courtroom procedures
   b. the courtroom is a miniature social world where people think about and influence each other
   c. the study of criminal cases can provide important new insight into the causes of aggression and conflict
   d. social psychology had its roots in the study of the courtroom

3. What percentage of criminal cases, disposed of in Canadian courts, come to trial?
   a. 15
   b. 25
   c. 50
   d. 75

4. Jurors who were asked to observe and evaluate eyewitnesses to the staged theft of a University of Alberta calculator
   a. believed both correct and incorrect eyewitnesses most of the time
   b. were suspicious of both correct and incorrect eyewitnesses
   c. believed the correct eyewitnesses but were suspicious of the incorrect eyewitnesses
   d. were suspicious of incorrect female eyewitnesses but tended to believe incorrect male eyewitnesses

5. Research suggests that eyewitnesses who correctly remember trivial details surrounding a crime
   a. also have a better memory for the culprit's face
   b. have a poorer memory for the culprit's face
   c. are less susceptible to misleading questions
   d. are more susceptible to misleading questions

6. Studies of the impact of eyewitness testimony indicate that
    a. eyewitnesses who have been discredited have no influence on a jury's judgments
    b. when witnessing conditions are shown to have been poor, jurors usually do not believe the eyewitness testimony
    c. eyewitnesses who are shown to have poor eyesight have no effect on the jurors' judgments
    d. none of the above are true

7. When students were presented with a hypothetical robbery-murder with circumstantial evidence but no eyewitness testimony, only 18 percent voted for conviction. With the addition of eyewitness testimony to the circumstantial evidence,
    a. the majority of students voted for conviction provided the eyesight of the eyewitness was not called into question
    b. the majority of students voted for conviction even if the eyesight of the eyewitness was called into question
    c. 35 percent of the students voted for conviction provided the vision of the eyewitness was not called into question
    d. even fewer students voted for conviction if the eyesight of the witness was shown to be very poor

8. Eric and Patricia were in a Rogers Video store when it was robbed. Who is more likely to give an accurate identification of the suspect?
    a. Patricia who has a vivid memory of the poster on the wall for the move "The Pianist"
    b. Eric who didn't notice any posters
    c. either witness will be equally accurate
    d. the person who has the better eyesight

9. Students at a university witnessed an assault on a professor. Seven weeks later when asked to identify the assailant from a group of six photographs,
    a. the majority made a wrong identification
    b. the majority chose the right person but distorted important details of the assault
    c. the majority of females chose the right person but the majority of males identified the wrong person
    d. seniors were more accurate than freshmen in identifying the assailant

10. Research on memory construction indicates that suggestive questioning can lead people to believe that
    a. yield sign was actually a stop sign
    b. a red light was actually green
    c. a robber had a moustache when he did not
    d. all of the above

11. A witness to a hit and run accident was asked if the car that took off was red. The witness now remembers that the car was red. This is an example of
    a. the problem of retelling the story
    b. suggestive questioning
    c. the misinformation effect
    d. both b and c

12. Which of the following witnesses is a jury most likely to believe?
    a. 11-year-old Sammy whose mother is a police officer
    b. Laura, a retired teacher
    c. Val, a sales person who is confident about what she saw
    d. José, a quiet spoken college business student

13. Research indicates that having eyewitnesses rehearse their answers to questions before taking the witness stand
    a. raises uncertainty in the minds of eyewitnesses as to what they actually saw
    b. increases their confidence about what they saw
    c. increases their confidence but also heightens their anxiety about appearing in court
    d. invariably leads them to give a much more detailed and accurate account of what they saw

14. Eyewitnesses who received confirming feedback on their testimony
    a. often felt manipulated and were less confident about their judgment
    b. recalled being more confident when making their initial judgment
    c. reported that the feedback significantly increased their confidence from when they made their initial judgment
    d. expressed greater liking for the experimenter and willingness to participate in additional research

15. Beth is an eyewitness to an assault that occurred outside her apartment building. According to the research, which of the following should make us more likely to believe that Beth's testimony is accurate?
    a. Beth picked the suspect out of a lineup when she was told the real perpetrator might not be in the lineup
    b. Beth is very certain that she saw the man and can report lots of details of the incident
    c. A professional psychologist testifies that she believes that Beth's testimony is reliable
    d. all of the above

16. Research has indicated that false lineup identifications can be reduced by
    a. having witnesses make individual yes/no judgments in response to a sequence of people
    b. reminding witnesses that the offender may not be in the lineup
    c. using a "blank" lineup that contains no suspects and screening out those who make false identifications
    d. all of the above

17. Whose eyewitness testimony is probably the most reliable?
    a. Theresa's report immediately after a bank robbery. She was simply asked by police to tell in her own words what happened.
    b. Cheryl's testimony about a grocery store hold-up. She has been interviewed eight times by the prosecuting attorney before appearing in court.
    c. David's testimony about a car accident. He has been interviewed three times by the defense attorney before his court appearance.
    d. Susan's report immediately after observing an attempted rape. She was asked very specific questions by the police, who believed they already had a suspect in custody.

18. When experts provide jurors information on the conditions under which eyewitness accounts are trustworthy
    a. jurors become more likely to trust such testimony
    b. jurors demonstrate reactance and are even more likely to accept inaccurate testimony
    c. jurors are not influenced by the information experts provide
    d. less intelligent jurors demonstrate reactance but more intelligent jurors analyze eyewitness testimony more carefully

19. Research comparing juries' decisions with those made by a judge has indicated that
    a. when a judge disagrees with the jury's decision it is usually because the jury convicts someone the judge would acquit
    b. juries generally recommend longer prison terms than judges are inclined to give
    c. two-thirds of the time the jury and the judge disagree
    d. four times in five the judge concurs with the jury's decision

20. Research on the physical attractiveness of defendants has indicated that physically attractive defendants are
    a. less likely to be found guilty and if found guilty receive less punishment
    b. less likely to be found guilty but if found guilty receive more punishment
    c. more likely to be found guilty and if found guilty receive more punishment
    d. more likely to be found guilty but if found guilty receive less punishment

21. Attorney Miller is defending Mary, a 20-year-old college student, who is being tried for failing to pay income tax. What should she do to boost Mary's chances of being acquitted?
    a. select Bill and Philip who are also college students to serve as jurors
    b. have Mary appear in court as attractively dressed as possible
    c. select young females as jurors
    d. she should do all of the above

22. Donald, a young mechanic, is on trial for a "date rape" sexual assault. According to the text, what juror is most likely to think he is guilty?
    a. a young female juror
    b. a young male juror
    c. a middle-aged male juror
    d. both the young male and female are equally likely to find Donald guilty

23. Someone accused of a crime is judged more sympathetically
    a. by females than by males
    b. if he or she appears to have personality characteristics that are complementary to a juror
    c. if he or she appears similar to a juror
    d. if there was a bystander who watched and did not intervene

24. Incriminating evidence that is heard in court but which is in face inadmissible
    a. rarely influences a jury's verdict
    b. only influences a jury if the Crown's case is weak
    c. does not influence a jury because the judge instructs the jurors to ignore such evidence
    d. usually has an influence on the jury

25. According to the text, a jury may demonstrate reactance in response to a
    a. dogmatic prosecuting attorney
    b. judge's instructions to ignore testimony
    c. self-confident eyewitness
    d. timid defense attorney

26. Which of the following is not part of the literature discussed in the text on social psychology and the courtroom?
    a. how the defendant's characteristics can influence jurors' judgments
    b. how the jurors' thought processes can influence their judgments
    c. how the physical environment of the jury room influences jurors' judgments
    d. how the judge's instructions influence jurors' judgments

27. In a study designed to test people's understanding of judicial instructions, viewers of videotaped instructions could answer _____ percent of the questions posed to them about what they had heard.
    a. 15
    b. 65
    c. 40
    d. 90

28. Statistical evidence given in court
    a. has a significant impact on the verdict
    b. is easily understood by judges and juries
    c. can have less impact than eyewitness testimony
    d. is rarely used by the defense

29. Jurors who are more prone to vote guilty tend to be
    a. more authoritarian
    b. lower in self-esteem
    c. from the upper socioeconomic class
    d. less authoritarian

30. Which of the following is true regarding the influence of minorities in jury deliberations?
    a. minorities composed of women are more influential than minorities composed of men
    b. frequently a minority view prevails and causes the majority to reverse its verdict
    c. a minority that favors acquittal stands a better chance of influencing the majority than does a minority that favors conviction
    d. minorities composed of high authoritarians are more influential than minorities composed of low authoritarians

31. What is meant by the "two-thirds-majority" scheme?
    a. two-thirds of all people asked refuse to serve on a jury
    b. two out of three times judges agree with the jury's decision
    c. a two-thirds majority is a better rule than consensus for a jury to follow in reaching a verdict
    d. the jury verdict is usually the alternative favored by at least two-thirds of the jurors at the outset

32. The fact that low authoritarians who initially recommended lenient punishments were even more lenient after group deliberation suggests that _____ can occur in juries.
    a. group polarization
    b. groupthink
    c. social facilitation
    d. reactance

33. Jurors who are male and of high social status
    a. are overrepresented on juries
    b. tend to be most influential in simulated juries
    c. tend to produce reactance in female jurors
    d. are most likely to disregard a judge's instructions

34. From research on minority influence we can speculate that jurors in the minority
    a. will never have a significant effect on the majority
    b. may be persuasive if they state their case tentatively
    c. may be persuasive if they are consistent and self-confident
    d. may be persuasive if they are females

35. Survey research findings report that _____ juries ultimately reach the verdict favored by the majority on the first ballot.
    a. 9 out of 10
    b. 5 out of 10
    c. 7 out of 10
    d. 3 out of 10

36. Attorney Johnson will be defending James S., who is accused of raping a 22-year-old woman. Who of the following jurors is likely to be least sympathetic to his client's case?
    a. John, a 40-year-old plumber who once served a sentence for burglary
    b. Todd, a 22-year-old college student who is a political liberal
    c. Wilma, a 42-year-old mother of two who tends to be authoritarian
    d. Rita, a 32-year-old television executive who opposes the death penalty

37. Jonas believes the accused is innocent. What can he do to convince other jurors to agree with him?
    a. state his views frequently
    b. remind the jury that eyewitness testimony is unreliable
    c. state his views once but very confidently
    d. Jonas shouldn't waste his time — the majority always wins

38. A twelve-member jury has heard all the evidence in a child abuse case and is beginning to deliberate. At the outset eight favour acquittal of the defendant and four favour conviction. Based on research in the text, the jury will probably
    a. be unable to reach a verdict and be a hung jury
    b. bring in a guilty verdict
    c. vote for acquittal
    d. vote for acquittal if the defendant is female and for conviction if the defendant is male

39. After hearing evidence in a murder trial, twelve jurors tend to believe the evidence is insufficient to convict the 25-year-old Black defendant. According to the group polarization hypothesis, after the jurors deliberate
    a. they will be more convinced the defendant is guilty
    b. they will be more convinced the evidence is insufficient to convict
    c. they will be evenly split with some convinced he is guilty and others convinced he is innocent
    d. they will be split with a minority favoring acquittal and the majority favoring conviction

40. According to the text, simulated juries
    a. can help us formulate theories we can use to interpret the more complex world
    b. are almost identical to real juries so that we can readily generalize from one to the other
    c. have been viewed by the majority of Supreme Court judges as valuable in predicting the behaviour of actual juries
    d. have mundane but not experimental realism

SHORT ESSAY QUESTIONS

Answer the following questions in the space provided.

1. Briefly explain how error may creep into eyewitness testimony

2. Explain how error in eyewitness testimony might be reduced.

3. Identify two defendant characteristics that may influence jurors' judgments.

4. Explain how a judge's instructions can create reactance.

5. Identify thought processes that can influence a juror's verdict.

6. Briefly give two examples of how juries are swayed by the same influences that bear upon other types of groups.

7. Discuss the value of simulated juries as well as their possible limitations.

ANSWER KEY

Chapter Review

1. influence

2. persuasive
   incorrect
   accuracy

3. memories
   Retelling
   please
   believe
   feedback

4. train
   false
   eyewitness

5. biases
   attractive
   similar
   evidence

6. inadmissible
   added
   emotional

7. evidence
   instructions
   verdicts

8. statistics
   memories
   clearer
   simple

9. 3
   95

10. two-thirds
    hung

11. consistent
    defections
    male
    high

12. strong
    lenient
    polarization
    stronger

13. more
    better
    informational

14. Simulated
    controlled
    courtroom

Matching Terms

1. i
2. k
3. f
4. l
5. d
6. j

7. c
8. g
9. b
10. e
11. h
12. a

True-False Review

1. T
2. F
3. T
4. F
5. F
6. T
7. T
8. T
9. T
10. T
11. T
12. F
13. T

14. F
15. F
16. F
17. T
18. T
19. F
20. T
21. F
22. T
23. T
24. F
25. F

Multiple-Choice Practice Test

1.	c	21.	d
2.	b	22.	a
3.	a	23.	c
4.	a	24.	d
5.	b	25.	b
6.	d	26.	c
7.	b	27.	a
8.	b	28.	c
9.	a	29.	a
10.	d	30.	c
11.	d	31.	d
12.	c	32.	a
13.	b	33.	b
14.	b	34.	c
15.	a	35.	a
16.	d	36.	c
17.	a	37.	a
18.	a	38.	c
19.	d	39.	b
20.	a	40.	a

MODULE C
SOCIAL PSYCHOLOGY AND THE SUSTAINABLE FUTURE

CHAPTER OBJECTIVES

After completing your study of this chapter you should be able to:

1. Discuss the nature of the global crisis.
2. Identify two different routes to sustainable lifestyles.
3. Describe the relationship between materialism and well-being.
4. Discuss how our capacity for adaptation and tendency to make social comparisons explain the psychology of consumption.
5. Explain psychology's potential contributions to a sustainable future.

CHAPTER REVIEW

Supply the words necessary to complete each of the following statements.

1. As we began a new millennium _____ news was bursting from all around. Food production had _____ in most Western countries and welfare rolls were _____ and inflation was_____.

THE GLOBAL CRISIS

2. However, this good news is only half the story. The earth has overshot its _____ carrying capacity. World _____ is projected to increase and economic growth is increasing _____.

3. One route to a sustainable future is through increasing technological _____ and agricultural _____. A second route is through reducing _____ and decreasing _____. For example, one proposal is to tax people on the basis of what they _____ rather than on the basis of what they _____

THE SOCIAL PSYCHOLOGY OF MATERIALISM AND SIMPLICITY

4. There is a tendency for wealthy nations to have more _____ people. However, in Canada, Europe, and the United States, the correlation between income and personal happiness is _____. Economic growth in affluent countries has provided no apparent boost to human _____.

259

5. One reason why materialism fails to continue to satisfy us is based on the principle of the _____ -level phenomenon—our tendency to adapt to a given level of _____ and react to changes from that level.

6. Much of life revolves around social _____. The frequent result of our tendency to compare upward is relative _____.

TOWARD SUSTAINABLE CONSUMPTION

7. More earth-friendly behaviour will result from public policies that give incentives for _____, from persuasive appeals that elicit _____ to specific behaviours, and from changing "me" thinking to "_____" thinking and present thinking to _____ thinking.

8. Recent values surveys suggest the beginnings of a decline in _____ values. There are signs of a new generation maturing with decreasing concern for economic _____ and an increasing concern for personal _____, the integrity of _____, and the meaning of _____.

9. Psychology's studies of the good life, point to the importance of _____ relationships, a hope-filled _____ , positive traits, and engaging _____.

MATCHING TERMS

Write the letter of the correct term from the right before the appropriate number on the left.

_____ 1. So absorbed in an activity we lose consciousness of self and time.

_____ 2. Preference for high income, occupational success and prestige.

_____ 3. The belief that there is a connection between wealth and well-being feeds this.

_____ 4. The frequent result of upward social comparison.

_____ 5. Natural resources that cannot sustain an increasing population.

_____ 6. The biologically productive space that people in different countries require to produce what they consume and to absorb their waste.

_____ 7. Elements of a genuinely good life.

_____ 8. Produced by cars and by the burning of coal and oil.

_____ 9. Our feelings of satisfaction and dissatisfaction are relative to our prior achievements.

a. adaptation-level phenomenon

b. "ecological footprints"

c. relative deprivation

d. flow

e. global crisis

f. Yuppie values

g. "cycle of work and spend"

h. greenhouse gases

i. close relationships, faith, engaging activity

TRUE-FALSE REVIEW

Circle T if the statement is true and F if it is false.

T F   1. Since 1960, world population has tripled while food production has only doubled.

T F   2. As we entered the new millennium, the price of cars, air travel, and hamburgers were at record inflation-adjusted lows.

T F   3. A century ago, the leading causes of death were accidents and cancer.

T F   4. In only a few countries have fertility rates dropped to replacement levels.

T F   5. Asians now buy more cars than Western Europeans and North Americans together.

T F   6. At the present rate of destruction, according to zoologist E. O. Wilson, half the earth's plant and animal species could be extinct within a century.

T F   7. The earth seems capable of permanently supporting five billion people consuming as do today's Western Europeans and North Americans.

T F   8. If everyone consumed like today's Americans and Canadians, the natural resources of three earths would be required.

T F   9. One route to a sustainable future is through increasing technological efficiency and agricultural productivity.

T F 10. Thanks to family planning efforts, the world's population growth rate has decelerated, especially in developed nations.

T F 11. To reduce consumption, Robert Frank proposes that we tax people on what they spend rather than on what they earn.

T F 12. Generally money can buy happiness.

T F 13. In poor countries, lower income people are less satisfied compared to higher income people.

T F 14. In Canada, Europe, and the U.S., the correlation between income and personal happiness is weak.

T F   15. Very rich people are significantly happier than the average person.

T F   16. People whose incomes have increased over the previous decade are happier than those whose income has not increased.

T F   17. Economic growth in affluent societies has provided no apparent boost to human morale.

T F   18. Based on research findings, individualism would encourage a greater sense of well-being.

T F   19. College alumni who prefer success and prestige to marriage are happier than their former classmates.

T F   20. People who believe society is too materialistic think it is not important to have a beautiful house and new car.

T F   21. The concept of relative deprivation refers to the perception that yesterday's luxuries are today's necessities .

T F   22. The adaptation-level phenomenon suggests that we can learn to adjust to a simplified way of living.

T F   23. Gallup reported that the need to experience spiritual growth has declined significantly in recent years.

T F   24. After watching depictions of the grim life in 1900, women expressed greater satisfaction with their own lives.

T F   25. Most people are happier gardening than power boating.

MULTIPLE-CHOICE PRACTICE TEST

Circle the correct letter.

1. Since 1960, _____ has increased and _____ have decreased.
   a. inflation-adjusted price of milk; drunken driving fatalities
   b. hard liquor consumption; inflation-adjusted prices of cars and hamburgers
   c. food production; welfare rolls
   d. the rate of inflation; stock market prices

2. In the last 50 years, _____ has increased.
   a. inflation
   b. carpooling
   c. affluence
   d. charitable contributions

3. Studies of world population indicate that
   a. fertility rates have dropped to replacement levels only in North America
   b. in developing countries birth rates have fallen too little to preclude rapid population growth
   c. world population is projected to reach 12 billion by 2050
   d. once replacement level birth rates are reached, world population immediately stops increasing

4. Exploding world population has resulted all of the following <u>except</u>
   a. impoverishment
   b. malnutrition
   c. famines
   d. illness

5. Global warming results in
   a. a reduction of greenhouse gases
   b. less rain than snow falling
   c. insects migrating toward the poles
   d. glaciers melting more slowly

6. Economic growth and increased consumption has been accompanied by increases in
    a. the polar ice caps
    b. forest cover
    c. droughts
    d. stocks of wild salmon and herring

7. Which of the following is an example of ecological toxicity?
    a. Bangladesh's population growth of 2.4 million per year
    b. the world's richest 20% eat twice as much meat today as they did in 1950
    c. the world's poorest 20% own 1% of the world's vehicles
    d. a family of 4 live in a 4000-square-foot house

8. Studies of economic growth and consumption indicate that
    a. Western Europeans and North Americans together buy more cars than the rest of the world combined
    b. global warming is causing the world's forest cover to increase dramatically
    c. at the present rate of destruction all the earth's plant and animal species will be extinct within a century
    d. the earth is capable of permanently supporting only two billion people consuming as do today's Western Europeans and North Americans

9. "Ecological footprints" refers to
    a. the destruction of animal life resulting from the loss of forest cover
    b. the biologically productive space people in different nations require to produce what they consume and to absorb their wastes
    c. the impact of ecosystem destruction on the stocks of the 10 major fish species
    d. the worldwide impact of both beneficial and destructive human activity on the physical and social environment

10. Canadians require the equivalent of about _____ soccer fields of biologically productive space per person to produce what they consume and to absorb their waste.
    a. 2
    b. 8
    c. 4
    d. 10

11. The text suggests that plausible future technologies include
    a. cars that run on water
    b. washing machines that consume no water, heat, or soap
    c. edible plants that require no nutrients to grow
    d. shoes and clothes that never show wear

12. If birth rates everywhere immediately fell to replacement levels,
    a. population growth would also immediately stop
    b. total population would immediately begin a slow decline
    c. total population would immediately begin a rapid decline
    d. population growth would still continue for years to come

13. Birth rates have fallen where
    a. food security has improved and women have become educated and empowered
    b. employment has increased and inflation has decreased
    c. food prices have stabilized and hard liquor consumption has been controlled
    d. males are better educated and materialism declines

14. Economist Robert Frank proposes that we reduce consumption by taxing people on what they
    a. sell
    b. spend
    c. earn
    d. weigh

15. All of the following are public policies to reduce consumption except
    a. subsidizing mass transportation
    b. rewarding recycling
    c. refunding the deposit on soda cans
    d. providing a monetary bonus for having children (previously called a "baby bonus")

16. The "cycle of work and spend" refers to
    a. working hard but spending more
    b. working less but spending less
    c. working more to spend more
    d. working less, spending less, but feeling happier

17. Research on national wealth and well-being indicates that
    a. the Bulgarians are happier than the Irish
    b. in poor countries, such as India, being relatively well off does not predict greater well-being
    c. the Swiss and Scandinavians are generally prosperous but unhappy
    d. in affluent societies, where most can afford life's necessities, affluence shows very little relationship to personal happiness

18. A survey of the Forbes 100 wealthiest people found that they are _____ happy than average.
    a. significantly more
    b. slightly less
    c. slightly more
    d. significantly less

19. Compared to their grandparents, today's young adults have grown up with
    a. greater happiness
    b. fewer social pathologies
    c. less affluence
    d. greater depression

20. College alumni who preferred a high income and occupational success and prestige to having very close friends and a close marriage were twice as like as their former classmates to describe themselves as "fairly" or "very"
    a. unhappy
    b. introverted
    c. happy
    d. extroverted

21. When Robert Frank served as a volunteer in rural Nepal he
    a. felt wealthy because of his monthly stipend
    b. felt impoverished because of his monthly stipend
    c. suffered for a long time because of his changed standard of living
    d. quickly adapted to his changed standard of living

22. Compared to those who lived a century ago, people today are more likely to declare themselves

    a. happier
    b. less happy
    c. more depressed
    d. less depressed

23. The two principles that help explain why people are not happier after attaining greater wealth are

    a. flow and relative deprivation
    b. social comparison and flow
    c. the adaptation-level phenomenon and social comparison
    d. the adaptation-level phenomenon and displacement

24. The tendency to adapt to a given level of stimulation and thus to notice and react to changes from that level is

    a. relative deprivation
    b. the adaptation-level phenomenon
    c. ecological footprints effect
    d. social comparison

25. What personal trait has been positively related to happiness?

    a. self-esteem
    b. conscientiousness
    c. introversion
    d. passivity

26. A 65-degree day seems warm in February but cold in July. This is best explained in terms of

    a. relative deprivation
    b. displacement
    c. the adaptation-level phenomenon
    d. social comparison

27. After Tim won one million dollars in the state lottery, he was ecstatic. After a year, however, his sense of life satisfaction returned to what it was before he won. This change in Tim's feelings can best be explained in terms of
    a. relative deprivation
    b. the adaptation-level phenomenon
    c. flow
    d. opponent-process theory

28. Our tendency for social comparison frequently results in
    a. the adaptation-level phenomenon
    b. flow
    c. relative deprivation
    d. communal "we" thinking

29. Compared to others, victims of paralyzing accidents
    a. typically experience a significant and lasting loss of life satisfaction
    b. eventually recover a normal or near-normal level of life satisfaction
    c. experience a highly fluctuating sense of psychological well-being throughout the rest of life.
    d. eventually experience a higher sense of self-esteem but a lower sense of relatedness to others

30. After a baseball player signs for $12 million a year, a $7 million teammate who has equal skill is most likely to experience
    a. flow
    b. reaction formation
    c. relative deprivation
    d. projection

31. Maria was happy with her grade of "C" on her social psychology test until she learned that all her classmates received "A's" or "B's." The shift in Maria's feelings is best explained in terms of
    a. dissatisfaction effect
    b. reaction formation
    c. the adaptation-level phenomenon
    d. relative deprivation

32. Gallup reported that the desire to connect to things larger than _____ is growing.

    a. one's self
    b. others
    c. God
    d. Humankind

33. The text suggests that more earth-friendly behaviour will arise from changing _____ thinking to _____ thinking.

    a. pessimistic; optimistic
    b. analytical; holistic
    c. future; present
    d. "me"; "we"

34. According to the text, a blossoming turn-of-the-century social ecology movement is promoting

    a. education on "Killer Thoughts for a World with Limits"
    b. "present" thinking over "future" thinking
    c. the return of mental hospital patients to community living
    d. an increase in the size of each society's "ecological footprints"

35. Marshall Dermer found that after women imagined and wrote about being burned and disfigured they

    a. became deeply depressed
    b. were more responsive to a request for help
    c. expressed greater satisfaction with their own lives
    d. experienced a significant loss in personal control

36. Csikszentmihalyi found that people are most likely to experience flow when

    a. unself-consciously absorbed in a mindful challenge
    b. involved in a passive leisure activity that requires little thought
    c. involved in intense interpersonal conflict with a close relative
    d. passing from the state of wakefulness to sleep

37. Most people are happier when _____ than when _____.

    a. talking to friends; watching TV
    b. watching TV; talking to friends
    c. power boating; gardening
    d. watching TV; power boating

38. People are much likelier to declare themselves "very happy" if they
    a. are highly educated
    b. are physically attractive
    c. have intimate friendships
    d. have many children

39. Wilbert's leisure activities include watching television, woodcarving, power boating, and sitting alone in the woods. Research suggest he is most likely to experience "flow" when
    a. daydreaming in the woods
    b. woodcarving
    c. power boating
    d. watching television

40. Michelle is a saleswoman who is depressed because recently she was denied a promotion. To increase her happiness with life, Michelle should
    a. imagine what her life would be like if she lost her job
    b. compare her life with the co-worker who actually received the promotion
    c. recall moments from her early childhood when she was very happy
    d. identify the negative qualities of her supervisor who denied the promotion

SHORT ESSAY QUESTIONS

Answer the following questions in the space provided.

1. Briefly describe the causes of the present global crisis.

2. Discuss two different routes to sustainable lifestyles.

3. Cite the evidence for increased materialism and describe the relationship between wealth and well being.

4. Briefly explain the adaptation-level phenomenon and relative deprivation.

5. Identify the factors that seem to be associated with a genuinely good life.

ANSWER KEY

Chapter Review

1. good
   tripled
   shrinking
   low

2. ecological
   population
   consumption

3. efficiency
   productivity
   consumption
   population
   spend
   earn

4. satisfied
   weak
   morale

5. adaptation
   stimulation

6. comparison
   deprivation

7. conservation
   commitments
   we
   future

8. materialist
   growth
   relationships
   nature
   life

9. close
   faith
   activity

Matching Terms

1. d
2. f
3. g
4. c
5. e

6. b
7. i
8. h
9. a

True-False Review

1. F
2. T
3. F
4. F
5. T
6. T
7. F
8. T
9. T
10. T
11. T
12. F
13. T

14. T
15. F
16. F
17. T
18. F
19. F
20. F
21. F
22. T
23. F
24. T
25. T

Multiple-Choice Practice Test

1.	c	21.	d
2.	c	22.	b
3.	b	23.	c
4.	c	24.	b
5.	c	25.	a
6.	c	26.	c
7.	b	27.	b
8.	d	28.	c
9.	b	29.	b
10.	d	30.	c
11.	b	31.	d
12.	d	32.	a
13.	a	33.	c
14.	b	34.	a
15.	d	35.	c
16.	c	36.	a
17.	d	37.	a
18.	c	38.	c
19.	d	39.	b
20.	a	40.	a